SWITCH: THE COMPLETE CATULLUS

Switch: The Complete Catullus

Isobel Williams

CARCANET CLASSICS

First published in Great Britain in 2023 by
Carcanet
Alliance House, 30 Cross Street
Manchester, M2 7AQ
www.carcanet.co.uk

A CIP catalogue record for this book is
available from the British Library.

ISBN 978 1 80017 339 2

Book design by Andrew Latimer, Carcanet
Typesetting by LiteBook Prepress Services
Printed in Great Britain by SRP Ltd, Exeter, Devon

The publisher acknowledges financial
assistance from Arts Council England.

For the riggers and the models

With thanks to Hubert Best, Dr Sarah Cullinan Herring, Dr Tristan Franklinos, Professor Stephen Harrison; Taki Kodaira for calligraphy instruction; Meredith McKinney for Japanese translation; Jill Ferguson and Violet Hill for Latin teaching; the editors of *Blackbox Manifold, Envoi, The Frogmore Papers, PN Review, Poetry Salzburg Review* and *Stand* where some of these poems were first published. A selection also featured in the Carcanet anthology *New Poetries VIII*.

Photography by Dick Makin Imaging, dmimaging.co.uk.

The Propertius epigraph is taken from S.J. Heyworth's Oxford Classical Texts edition (2007).

Read 'em and weep, the dead man's hand again.
Ace of Spades, Motörhead

libertas quoniam nulli clam restat amanti,
  liber erit, viles si quis amare volet.

Lovers have no freedom now.
  To be free, abandon love.
Propertius II, 23

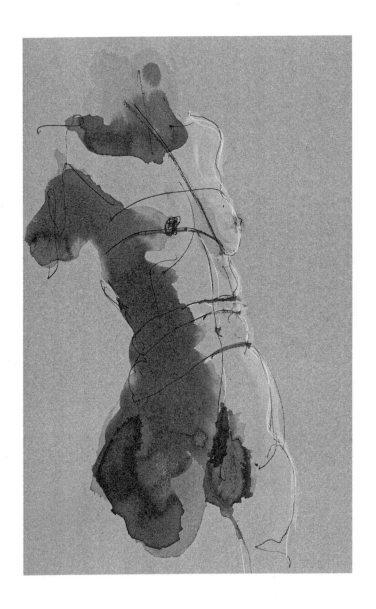

Catullus controls several poetic metres. From poem 65 onwards he uses only the elegiac couplet: dactylic hexameter, then dactylic pentameter. Six feet out, five feet back. Rise, fall, lead, follow, a form for a switch. Catullus splits into an anxious bitchy dominant with the boys, a howling submissive with his nemesis, the older woman he calls Lesbia.

In Japan, the English word has been adopted with its street meaning: these rope hiragana characters say *suittchi*.

CONTENTS

1

This book belongs to _____

                    misappropriated
Words glistening raw, vellum exfoliated –
Yours if you want to navigate its folds,
Diving for cargo in the drowned holds.

Tell the teachers dead and alive I'm sorry.
While they were splitting Gaul in three they knew
I'd waste a lifetime waiting for the ferry.

Drop in. Whatever. Take a generous view.
This house dust/book dust will grow damp with tears
If I outlive him, cursed with my hundred years.

I draw Japanese rope bondage (shibari) as an outsider. What I see is created for an audience, with the consent of all parties. No! I am not Miss Whiplash, nor was meant to be.

Catullus was held in emotional bondage by affairs with men and women. The Roman Republic knew nothing of the Japanese archipelago: I use shibari simply as a context.

Shibari ('binding') is derived from the ancient martial art of hojōjutsu. A dominant top, or rigger, ties a submissive, also called a bottom, model or bunny. Performers start with floorwork. The rigger may then suspend the bottom in a sequence of transitions, communicating via breaths and glances. Theatrical elements can include dripping wax on skin (the candles used have a low melting point).

There is a fluid dynamic with a constant flicker of role-reversal. Gorgone, a French star of tying and being tied, describes the paradox of who's really in charge: being a top is about humility, being a bottom is about power.

When tied, Gorgone feels like the golem, the formless creature of clay given shape when the Hebrew word אמת (*emet*, truth) is written on her forehead. The rigger's vision creates her in rope. 'I was nothing and your eyes saw me,' she says.

Thine eyes did see my substance, yet being unperfect; and in thy book all my members were written, which in continuance were fashioned, when as yet there was none of them.

Psalm 139, verse 16

Shibari is a form of translation. The top arranges the bottom in a shape he or she could not hold or maybe even attain alone.

In Shakespeare's *A Midsummer Night's Dream*, Bottom temporarily has an ass's head when he is ensnared in Oberon's quasi-shibari public domination of his wife Titania. Translators must try to avoid giving a text the head of a donkey through misreading or doubtful taste, but at least they do no permanent harm to the original. Rope marks on the skin should leave a pleasing pattern but will soon fade.

Side-stepping one problem, my versions here are not (for the most part) literal translations, but take an elliptical orbit around the Latin, brushing against it or defying its gravitational pull.

BELINDA: Ay, but you know, we must return good for evil.
LADY BRUTE: That may be a mistake in the translation.
Sir John Vanbrugh, *The Provok'd Wife*

Catullus gets under the skin. You suffer with him if you meet him in the schoolroom: all that wounded self and thwarted desire.

He collars you with urgent clarity (what Robert Herrick calls his 'terse muse'). Vital and volatile, elegant and cruel, he is a learned master of poetic form who covers the range: beauty, anguish, tender lyrics, spite; low-life drama, glittery wedding poems, street encounters, sweeping myth; love laid bare in all its moods; and vengeful smutty attacks – a streak of powered-up *Viz* without the good intentions.

Facts about Gaius Valerius Catullus are scarce. His life, or a version of it, is in his poems. Here are some stepping stones to the present:

Circa 84 BC: Born into the minor aristocracy. His father, a citizen of Verona, has a villa on Lake Garda and knows Julius Caesar.

?? BC: Moves to Rome. This is the late Roman Republic, buffeted by rivals grabbing wealth and raising armies. Catullus thrives in a cultured elite. Makes friends and enemies.

Money: Complains about being broke but has private means (so needs no patron). Targets bankrupts and a love rival who can't afford slaves. A book-keeper's eye: 20.35% of his poems include numbers or counting.

Morals: Conflicted. Combines traditional Roman fastidiousness with a racy life which he mines for material, using real names. Targets shaggers, incestuous shaggers, politicians and plutocrats.

Boyfriend trouble: Jumpy and jealous over a sought-after Lord Alfred Douglas type called Juventius.

Woman trouble: Hangs out the love and hate in his excoriating affair with an older married aristocrat he names Lesbia, maybe to highlight her learning: the poetess Sappho was from Lesbos. Sometimes he calls her domina, the word a slave would use for his mistress.

If she exists, and as a woman, she might be Clodia Metelli, a politician's wife then widow. Whatever her deeds, trying to live as freely as an unfettered man of the time is enough to get this Clodia a bad rap. The orator Cicero implicates her in incest (with her brother Clodius) and even murder – is her husband's sudden death natural?

Poetry: Writes for a coterie, has an eye on posterity. Targets bad poets. Will be the leading survivor among the neoterics, a polished clique of new poets following Greek models, notably Callimachus who lived about two hundred years earlier. They discard the inimitably weighty Homeric epic for lyrics, elegies and epigrams on more personal themes, and the epyllion, an epic in miniature. Poetry doesn't yet rhyme but Catullus almost does at times, internally and at ends of lines (*angiportis/...nepotes*), building up the music with alliteration and assonance (*ave atque vale; tunditur unda*) and snatches of repetition.

?? BC: Bereavement: his cherished nameless brother dies in the Troad, the region where Troy stood in what is now Anatolia.

57–56 BC: Sampling politics, joins the retinue of Memmius, governor of the Roman province of Bithynia, now north-western Turkey. Is rude about him afterwards.

While on this tour, visits his brother's tomb. His lament for his brother (poem 101), full of plangent 'ah' sounds, ends with the lapidary *ave atque vale* (hail and farewell), a monument to the untranslatable and un-updatable.

By 54 BC: Accuses Julius Caesar, who is subduing Gaul and Britain, of lechery, sodomy, letting his chief engineer loot conquered lands, and (possibly the worst in Catullus's eyes) being a pseudo-intellectual. Gets away with it.

Circa 54 BC: Dies – or not – aged about twenty-nine (older than Keats, close to Marlowe). C.H. Sisson's 'the body burnt out by lechery' is not ascertainable. Will influence pillars of the canon, including Horace, Martial, Ovid, Propertius and Virgil, and disintegrate into mere fragments quoted by others.

9th century: A spark – poem 62 pops up in an anthology.

Circa 1300: Crashes through to posterity. A manuscript full of errors, from a time more recent than his, turns up in Verona. It is lost again, but not before being copied to start the chain reaction which draws in Petrarch. Poems 1-60 are short, in a variety of metres, with gaps left by three poems incorporated in the sixteenth century, rejected in the nineteenth. They are followed by seven longer poems, a compact epic and forty-eight epigrams. Scholars debate whether Catullus assigned the poems' order. All I know is that when I rearranged them into boy poems and girl poems it looked like a dog's breakfast.

1472: Printed for the first time, in Venice. Catullus scholarship gets going.

1570s: Has been echoed by other English poets, but translation into English kicks off with Sir Philip Sidney and poem 70; pitch invasion starts about 200 years later.

1680: Jean de La Chapelle begins the novelisation of Catullus with *Les Amours de Catulle*, while maintaining that he is writing 'des conjectures Historiques'.

18th and 19th centuries: Catullus and Lesbia are subjects for paintings and engravings which celebrate pretty people in drapery.

1943: First performance of Carl Orff's cantata *Catulli Carmina* for tenor, soprano, chorus and percussion.

1969: C.H. Sisson calls Catullus 'my friend across twenty centuries', an easy mistake to make about someone so compelling but so judgemental.

1972–94: Cy Twombly paints *Untitled (Say Goodbye, Catullus, to the Shores of Asia Minor)*, a vast abstract misquotation from poem 46 which has not shores but *campi* (plains). For a while Twombly calls it *Anatomy of Melancholy*.

2010: Anne Carson's *Nox* (night, also death) makes a reasonable bid for *ave atque vale* dominance with the infinite archaism 'farewell and farewell'.

2019: Let social media judge. 'Catullus: cried during sex' – @ala_Camillae, Twitter

SWITCH: THE COMPLETE CATULLUS

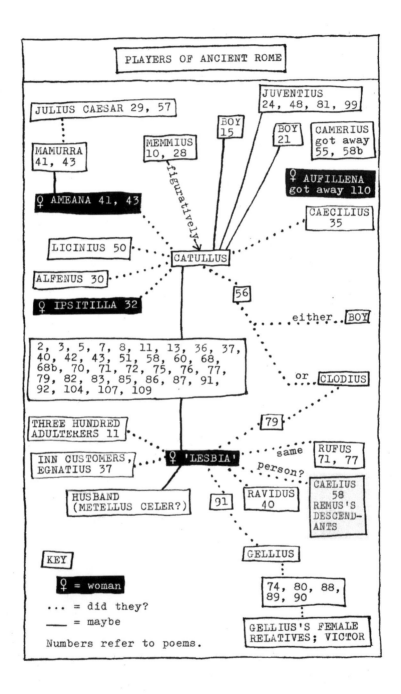

PLAYERS OF ANCIENT ROME

JULIUS CAESAR 29, 57

JUVENTIUS 24, 48, 81, 99

BOY 15

BOY 21

MEMMIUS 10, 28

MAMURRA 41, 43

CAMERIUS got away 55, 58b

♀ AUFILLENA got away 110

♀ AMEANA 41, 43

figuratively

CAECILIUS 35

LICINIUS 50

CATULLUS

ALFENUS 30

♀ IPSITILLA 32

56

either BOY

2, 3, 5, 7, 8, 11, 13, 36, 37, 40, 42, 43, 51, 58, 60, 68, 68b, 70, 71, 72, 75, 76, 77, 79, 82, 83, 85, 86, 87, 91, 92, 104, 107, 109

or CLODIUS

THREE HUNDRED ADULTERERS 11

79

INN CUSTOMERS, EGNATIUS 37

♀ 'LESBIA'

same person?

RUFUS 71, 77

HUSBAND (METELLUS CELER?)

91

RAVIDUS 40

CAELIUS 58 REMUS'S DESCENDANTS

GELLIUS

KEY

♀ = woman

... = did they?

—— = maybe

Numbers refer to poems.

74, 80, 88, 89, 90

GELLIUS'S FEMALE RELATIVES; VICTOR

Did they or didn't they? Dots show uncertainty. Lines, slightly less uncertainty. Clockwise from south-west of Catullus: he begs the prostitute Ipsitilla for a slot, calls Alfenus a traitor, languishes after poetry-making with Licinius, insults Ameana – but is there any action? (Licinius is the Calvus of 14, 53 and 96.)

Ameana's boyfriend, dismissed by Catullus as a bankrupt from the coastal town of Formiae, is thought to be Julius Caesar's extravagant chief engineer Mamurra. Catullus presents Mamurra as a corrupt fornicator partnered in crime with Caesar but apologises to the latter, according to Suetonius. Mamurra might be Catullus's hate-figure Mentula (penis) in 94, 105, 114 and 115.

Memmius (Catullus's boss on his lack-lustre stint of public service abroad) is only a metaphorical threat. Catullus's friends Aurelius and Furius don't clutter up the chart, but is hot toff Juventius the unnamed boy in 15 and/or 21 whom Aurelius is warned not to poach? Is Juventius's crush in 24 the hard-up Furius? Camerius seems to elude Catullus, as does Aufillena (who keeps the cash). Perhaps Caecilius is adored as a poet rather than love interest. Rufus might also be Caelius. This Gellius may be the one in 116.

In 56 Catullus claims that he mounted a boy. The text isn't clear: could the boy be his mistress Lesbia's slave or – if she is really Clodia Metelli – her brother, the demagogue Clodius Pulcher? Their incest might be implied in 79.

Catullus sometimes names her, but essence-of-Lesbia infuses other poems in which she is not named so I include those. I may be wrong to leave out 64 which is permeated with a sense of abandonment.

2

Oh little beak, how Mistress loves
To play with you and guard you in her nest,
Feed your craving with her fingertip,
Sharpen your need, make you nip hard –

She is the glowing core of my desire
But looks to you for flights of entertainment
And a fluttery release, we trust,
To let the tide of urgency subside.

I pray to uncage you as Mistress does
And make the crushing tortures of the soul
Lighter than a feather's stroke.

2 (B)

[?unrelated fragment]
Something something would be
As much relief to me
As sprinting girl in story found
When glinting quince untied the waste of years

3

Break, break, break, love gods and gorgeous people.
Mistress's little beak's been taken –
A consolation she was always petting
For the sheer love of the thing.

It knew Mistress as if she'd hatched it.
Rooted in her lap, it hopped about,
Cheeping just for Mistress.

Now it's submitted to that shady venture
From which no one returns to what they were.
Naughty creatures of the night, how could you –
Scoffing all the beautiful *objets d'art* –
You laid claim to my pretty little beak.

Oh how wicked. Poor little beak.
Now you're to blame for the state of Mistress's lovely
Eyes. Red-raw, tumescent, overflown.

4

Oh there was never another to touch her –
Yes, the drinks will be out in a minute –
Broad in the beam all right
But the fastest hull that flew and she knew it,
Flashing her stern at the boy
Racers from Thessaloniki
Under oars or canvas,

All logged here:
The Adriatic coast ('lethal'),
The Cyclades, your famous Rhodes,
The Sea of Marmara ('vicious north wind'),

The Black Sea shoreline ('horrific')
Where she grew up as trees,
Whispering adolescence with swishy hair,
Toes dug in the earth –

She swore her birth was watched
By pines and rippling box trees
High above Amastris and Cytorus –

She would paddle in their shallows
Then floated her master
Through cauldrons of hell,
Braced for buffeting from port or starboard
Or borne by even-handed winds of heaven

And never had to pray for safe harbour
From the ultimate sea to this millpond
Where she reminisces
In genteel decay

So pour a libation in her name
To the coxless pair Castor and Pollux

Then we'll go in and chat to the old dears
About the jolly boating weather.

5

Song of Snogs

Open out to life and love with me,
Clodia, and we'll set the regulators'
Hisses at the lowest rate of interest

Suns go down and dawns will come
But once our pinprick light is out
The night will never be for more than sleeping

I love doing this, let's
Take a long position, swell the Abacus with kisses
M Cxxx
MM CxCx Cxxx
MMM CxCx Cxxx CxCx

And when we've made a killing kissing
Shake the totals to lose count,
Take them beyond the kiss inspector's reach

6

Mr Gold:
Your latest pet must be witless and charmless
Or else you'd confide in Doctor Catullus.

So I'll tell you.
You've picked up some toxic tramp and you're ashamed.

Don't pretend you're filling in time with hand-jobs.
This bedroom's the crime scene –
Reeking of Lynx and sex-club lubricant.

Look, double-dented pillows
And this shuddering, juddering
Bed's got the staggers.

Come clean. That fuck-wasted look
Says you've done something regrettable.

Who is it?
Don't worry about my reaction.

To deal with my responses I make them public
In a disciplined explosion.

7

Stress-testing are we, Mistress?
How many of your tropes in rope
Can be endured before the poet chokes?

Ply me hemp silk jute and tie me
Ichinawa, takate kote,
Futomomo, hishi karada,
Tasuki, kannuki,
Hashira, daruma shibari.
All of it. Semenawa for the burn.

Count the stars that spy on sly
Lovers when the night is ball-gagged –

That's how many of your tight knots and rope marks
Will deliver me beyond madness –
More than a voyeur's torch could spot
Or a jealous sensei take to pieces.

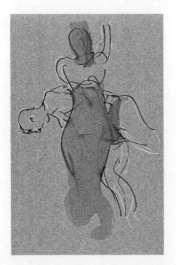

8

In tears again, Catullus. Just get out of bed.
Accept the past and have the loss adjusters in.
Oh, once upon a time you were the golden boy –
When you let Mistress use her harshest ropes on you.
You said you loved her more than all the rest blah blah.
She taught you how to show submissiveness and shame,
Following your instinct, and made you feel big.
The rumour was they even liked you in Japan.

So now she's dumped you and you can't get tied at will.
Don't chase vanilla boys or put your life on hold –
Try Buddhist meditation to endure the drought.

Mistress, get lost. Catullus-san's remade in stone.
He won't beg favours or come sniffing after you.
You'll pine for him now he's not snivelling in your wake.
What's promised for a has-been/never-was like you?
Who's next? Who's going to mumble that you're beautiful?
Who wants to feel the lash and be your slave by right?
Who'll let you kiss him, cut and bleeding in your ropes?

But you, Catullus – you're not even curious.

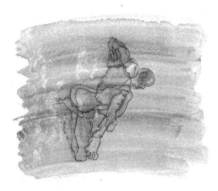

Metre: scazon

9

Veranius, my one chance in a thousand –

Did they lie? You're home
With your handsome brothers,
Your gorgeous mother?
I've waited so long and it's true.

Hold me spellbound again,
Wind your stories around me.
What are the Spanish boys like?

Let me embrace you without asking
Kiss you
Your beautiful mouth
Your eyes so beautiful
Wrap you like a present in my arms

However many men say they are blessed,
Don't I know joy and blessedness the most?

I will say the much the same
When she comes back to me
From blessing other men.
Do I feel it less then?

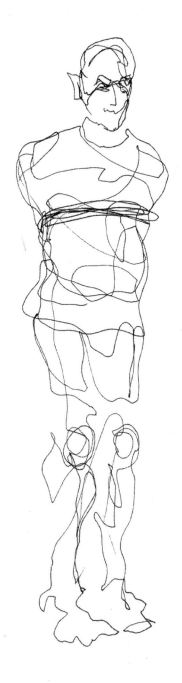

Hoist

Varus takes me to meet his new bondage model
At the rope jam while I'm idling –
A standard-issue whore's veneer
But *not without* some cheeky low appeal
So I use that distancing double negative
To pretend I don't fancy her.

We chat about my aberration –
The attempt at a job, my secondment to Tokyo
And whether I got a bonus.
I tell them straight – austerity minus for all,
Especially when your boss is too busy being fellated
Under the desk to look out for his team.

'But surely,' they chorus, 'you took time out at a
Dojo for advanced tuition?'
So, needing that girl to admire me, I say
(Look out for another double negative)
'I *wasn't* so busy with work that I *couldn't* pick up
Eight dynamic suspension transitions
Taught by a master' –

Although in fact there's no dojo on earth where I
Dare go beyond floorwork
In case the harness slips and strangles the bottom.
For aerial ties, I practise on
Myself, or chairs.

Now she hits me with some trollopy would-be posh act:
'Please tie me in all of them at the Seattle Erotic Art Festival
Next month, darling, it'll give me a competitive edge.'

'Hold on,' I tell the hardened little tramp,
'When I say "pick up" I mean
I watched the sensei teach them to my friend.
Yes he does exist and his name's Cinna.
All right, you call him Gaius, it's the same person.
The moves are all in my head, I just need
Time to work them out. But trust a
Clueless bloody parasite like you
To ignore the obvious interpretation.'

11

Be prepared

You two – you're my camp
Followers when I want to penetrate
The rim of India, surf-deafened beach-bum paradise,
Or nameless towns for soldiery and rent boys,
Or Parthia to be shot at by the locals.
We'll stain ourselves beside the delta waters
And thrust across the jutting Alps to spot
Caesar's crown jewels – the land of Lederhosen
And the last resort, Britain, where the rough trade
Parades in woad. You're braced for any road
Your luck might roll you down –

So take her this message, will you? Short and sour:

Goodbye. May God bless all who sail in you,
Three hundred Romeos at a time rammed in your
Hold. Forget romance. It's your obsessive
Quest to give them all a hernia.

Don't use my love as collateral.
It died, thanks to your little weakness, like
The elusive flower slashed by the
Combine harvester.

ROSALIND: But, for the bloody napkin?
OLIVER: By and by.

Shakespeare, *As You Like It*

Asinius, before I pin
A tail on you, I have to ask:

What personal item did you steal,
Up to your tricks as usual,
In breach of etiquette
With your sly left hand
When we were all stoned?
My Gucci earphones,
A sex toy, a rent boy,
A broken e-cigarette?

My stash? My studded leather
Harness? My suspender
Belt? My vintage Fender?
Larceny isn't clever –
Ask your smarter brother
Pollio: he's all set
To pay your criminal debt

So here's my standard threat –
A fire-hose of public abuse
Or return that souvenir
Of Spain from my own dear
Fabullus and Veranius.
I require it now
As much as I need my pet
Veranius, and Fabullus.

It's what someone like you
Calls a serviette.

13

We'll have an engorgement party on my sofas
So see you next Tuesday if you're lucky, Fabullus –
As long as you bring the sushi,
A user-friendly sub, some coke, Doritos
And jokes that are actually funny.

Yes, comrade, those are my house rules –
The poet's credit card is frayed at the edges

But I'll repay you with
The essential aphrodisiac,
Mistress's secretions straight from heaven.
One dab behind the ears and you'll comprehend
The naso-genital reflex theory.

14

You owe me a massive apology
For sending this crap anthology
When I was stuck
With no one to
Really Calvus
If I didn't love you beyond reason
I'd hate you with the zeal
Of that guy you put in jail.
What did I say or do to make you
Palm these terrible poets off on me?

And it's regifted. You've torn out the title page.
May boils afflict the grateful client
Who gave you this offence to humanity.
If, as I suspect, this novelty item
Comes from that pedagogue/pedant/pederast Sulla,
It's no skin off my nose
And I'm glad he recognised your labours
At their true worth

But what a godawful book
To inflict on your Catullus,
Stuck with the old dears for Christmas
Needing more than *Hard Times*.

The joke's on you, petal.
As soon as they're open
I'll scrape the complete jerks off the shelves –
That's C____, A____ and S____
In case you're wondering –
And get them gift-wrapped for you in revenge.

Now cheerio you lot. Hobble off back to the
Charity shop on your blistered poetical feet –
Blots on the backlist, bastard bards.

Next year, darling,
Just slip a book token in my stocking.

14 (B)

If you should read my muddy pearls
And not spit out your Viennese whirls
Bristling because it's boys not

15

Mr Blond, commending
Unto you this day
Myself and the love of my dreams,
Here's the deal:
If you've ever pined
To touch the hem of innocence
Guard him with good grace.

It isn't the crowd that concerns me –
I'm not afraid of your lackeys,
They keep off the grass –
But you and your dick, preying on
Boys of all persuasions.
Plant it where you like
Away from your own front door

But if malice or madness
Goad your criminal urge
To offend against my interests
Nemo me impune
Lacessit. You'll pay damages
Splayed out, strung up, receiving
Through your undefended porthole
Radishes for roughage and
Acanthopterygii –
Fish with spiny rays,

Primitive Perciformes
Like you.

16

Sweet

Beware the mighty sodomite face-bandit.
You two batty-boys dishing out lit crit
Insist my kissy-fit verse is Hello Kitty.

Look, being the guardian of what's good
Is work for the poet, not for the poet's works.
Liberation from your taste police
Gives my words a musky allure that can stir

Not just boys but the prick-memory
Of shaggy old ex-shaggers.

So writing kiss poems is an unmanly feat?
First line, repeat. XX

17

Yeah so feeling a connection here,
The revenge fantasy and my home town –
How you'd love a good long bridge
To prance around on,
Ready for the Verona Morris Men
Jigging up and down
But given the state of what you've got
You're right to fear a shiver of second-hand timbers,
Splattered legs in the air, slotted in sludge
To a curdled accordion wail

So may you get the new-build of your dreams
Fit for the jingling hobby-horse
But do you know what would give me a good laugh first?
A certain council-tax payer gets chucked over the side
In a backflip,
Misses the nice bit,
Plops deep in the putrid glutinous stink pit –
He'll do for the green man

Lacking the intellectual sweep of a two-year-old
Napping in doddery dad's toddler sling

And here we go, the sex interest, his wife,
Really up for it, not much more than a kid,
Should be under tighter guard from thievery
Than a Grand Cru vineyard ready to burst.
He doesn't even adjust his comb-over
But lets her flit around – this sad git halfwit
Sits it out to wonder what day it is
Like a Ford Transit totalled in a ditch.

Let me pitch him off arse over tit –
Will his reflex, turbocharged by shit,
Leave his passive instincts in the sucking
Ooze where pack-mules cast their iron shoes –

Time up already?   I was just getting
Going.   Thank you
Too.   See you next week.

21

Mr Blond, the all-devouring
All-time champion of feeding on demand –

You want the freedom of my boyfriend's arse.
You're all over him, private jokes, the lot.

No deal. When you try to outflank me
I'll force-feed you a deep-throat dinner.

If you marched on a full stomach I'd say nothing,
But I'm scared you'll teach my pet your scrounging appetites

So hands off, while you can without a scandal –
Unless you want a mouthful that chokes you to death.

22

Poets cornered, Varus.
Take that Suffenus of yours –
Poised, polished, pointed. Like us, you might say.

But prolific. At least ten thousand lines of the stuff.
And –
     pay attention, this is how we did it –

He won't scratch letters on a beeswax tablet
Or start on a palimpsest – used surfaces,
Old words ghosted –

But picks a fresh scroll,
Top-grade papyrus, fancy new wooden ends,
Crimson leather laces, parchment jacket,
Leaded straight lines, all roughness pumiced away –

And when it's unrolled
You'll see (drumroll)
Our nice Mister Suave
Has scuffed it with his muddy hooves.
How can such elegance clatter into a ditch?
This arbiter of wit
Yodels like a yokel
When he dips his special poetry pen –
Yet his greatest joy is to versify
Dazed by wonder at his art.

He's all of us, Varus.
Suffenus unto the day
We star in our own poetry snuff movie
But don't feel failure's claws hooked in our back.

23

Furius,
No housekeeper, no panic room, no heating,
Too arid for your home-loving arachnid,
Even the bedbugs voted with their feet.
Just your father and stepmother
Munching granite, cosy innit.
Daddy, eh, getting splinters from his wife.

No surprise, then –
You're all in good nick with iron digestions,
Free from worry in your no-comfort zone,
No house fire/freezer breakdown/aggravated
Burglary/neighbours pissing in your tank
Nor any other threat to the no-claims bonus.

The glare through curtainless windows, chilly draughts
And very low calorie diet
Desiccate you like silica gel.
How can you not be happy?
No sweat/saliva/mucus issue/toilet tissue,
Anal sphincter cleaner than a
Brushed steel salt cellar,
You shit less than once a month.
It's like dried beans or loose chippings but harder.
Rub the grounds – no stain on your hands.

Rich dividends, Furius, not to be discounted,
So please stop whining after that hundred grand loan:
You despise liquidity.

24

Ancestors blossom
At last in you. When you fall
All sweetness dies out,

Juventius, and I'd rather you buried him in
Great stinking piles of money
Than let him trail his ropes across your skin.
He is no Master
And he's broke.

'Why? Isn't he nice?' Oh not again.
Yes, nice enough for a man who's not a Master,
And broke.

Spin it any way you like

But he's no Master
And he's broke

25

Duck and dive

Oh and Thallus
You're a ponce
A fluffy bunny's tail
A mere smear of foie gras
A teeny-tiny downy unpierced earlobe
An old limp willy
Sooty wafty cobwebs but also Thallus
You scoop up stolen goods like a tornado
When birds on the wire are the worse for wear

So give me back that Loro Piana cashmere coat you nicked
It was a present from Mummy
The Spanish napkin of *huge* sentimental value
And my Balenciaga bathrobe you chancer
All of which you prance around in
Even though they don't suit you
Especially the napkin
Now peel them off your sticky claws
Or else I'll have incriminating weals
Etched on your lambkin bottom and thieving paws
And toss you off
(Wait for it)
Your silly blow-up giraffe
At the deep end
Because it's your fault you can't swim

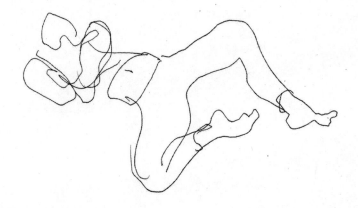

26

Furius,
That charming rectory
Has minimised stamp duty
And even avoided chancel repair liability
But the interest-only mortgage, flood plain
And negative equity
Will blow your house down.
You should have asked my father.

27

Gateway to heaven

Tell the boy on the snow white horse to deliver it.
The dictator's daughter recommends you.
She's in charge and
Sunk as a punch-drunk punked punk skunk on the junk.

Don't go cutting it with baby powder.
I'll pay for the good stuff.
It muzzles the bad thoughts.
People who expected something else
Are asking for a smack so they can stick
Their chateau-bottled up themselves.

28

In a state

Piso's team, famished for deals –
Got your visas and bags on wheels?
Well, Veranius and Fabullus,
What's the plan? Seen enough of
Failed disaster capitalism?
Any small change down the sofa?
My boss makes me enter debt
As credit – oh I've been well shafted
On the spreadsheet, Memmius –
You misheard bonus as boners.

Lads, we're level: you've been totalled
By a prick of equal standing.
Pick good mentors! Hope they get
Banged up by the regulators,
Pair of gilt-edged alligators.

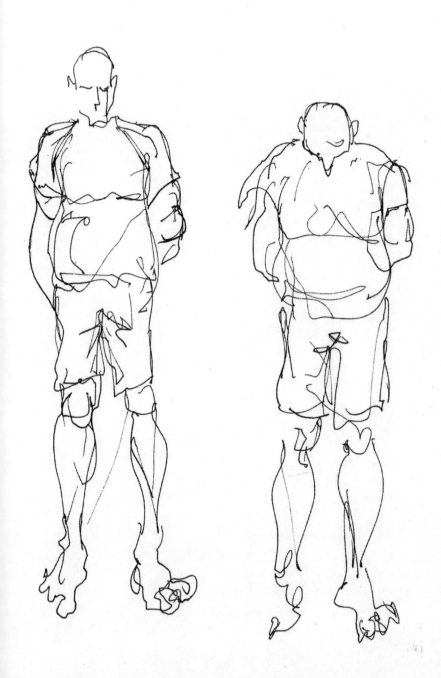

29

You bet I'm claiming a tax rebate.

Who can look at your shambles of a
Government without weeping?
Only a greedy chancer with no shame.

Mister Marble Balls himself
Greased his offshore accounts
With European subsidies,
Now he raids the British
And you, world ponce, you let it all go by?

Waggling his superfluous superego
He bedhops like a randy pigeon
Under a sex-god delusion
And you, world arse, you rubber stamp the lot?
You're that shameless greedy chancer.

Turning to the dildo king:
Was it for this you shafted
The islanders in the west –
To let your knackered fuckboy suck up billions?
Funny kind of overseas aid.

When will he reach the end of his shag-and-grab?
He's ripped through the family silver,
Helped himself in assorted tax havens,
Tanked economies, trashed Britain.
Why do you promote this shit?
What's his game plan? Looting pensions?

Was it for this your father- and son-in-law[1]
Act from the pillaging classes left us in ruins?

I'll send a fair sum. Sue me for the rest.

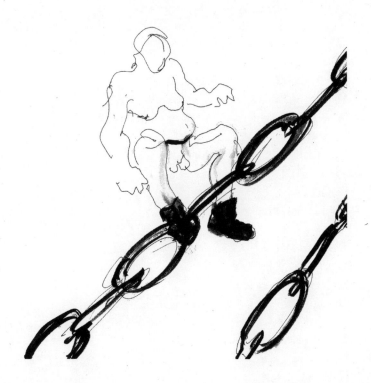

---

1   Julius Caesar and Pompey, allegedly

30

Ah! perfido

Alfenus. Stirrer, traitor, heart macerator,
False-flag planter, ironclad stone-heart bastard.
Happy now you've let me down?
No regret for my lost embrace?

Treachery won't get you likes and followers.
You left me washed up on my rocky island.
Where should the loyal long-term investor look now?

I'm mastered by your inkblot pupils spreading
As you close in for your on-centre
Perfect kiss
Cupid's bow cruelty

Then I'm blocked
Everything you did and said
Howled down by winds
Deleted from the cloud

Trade Nebulas all you want
Lashed to cryptocurrency
Facts will find you out
Holding counterfeit

31

Sirmione, my freshwater pearl
Of all the islands and the nearly islands
Seeded by the gods of sweet and salt
In clear lakes and interminable seas –
My spirit floats when I catch sight of you.

I can't believe I've left the plains of drudgery
And reached you safely. What's more delectable
Than to dump my shackles, free my thoughts
And – released from duty to make friends
Abroad – come home to be tucked up in bed?
It makes my intolerable ordeal worthwhile.

Mother of all mothers of pearl, Sirmione,
Take joy from joy restored to the young waster,
Let the ripples echo the lakeside laughter.

32

It's from Catullus. Pleeease, he says,
Blah blah darling, you're so hot,
So talented –
He wants my after-lunch slot,

A firm booking with no one else
Looking. He says if I stay
In the camera's eye
And concentrate
He'll come nine times

In that weird way of his.
You know he calls it 'fucktuations', right?
Now it's urgent, have I got
A cancellation? He's full of carbs,
Adopting the position

And here it is.
Look away now.
The dick pic.

33

Dear Membership Secretary

Time to deal with that changing-room arch-pilferer
Vibennius and his batty-boy brat –
Paternal paws are sticky,
Son's sphincter isn't picky.

Why not cancel their family membership?
Let them try that five-star dump next door.

After all, dad's pillaging's well known
And the lad can't sell his hairy bottom here
Even at trade prices
Any more.

34

Blessed Diana's girls intact
the pregnant one sacked
school song sung lesson bells rung
Dian's bud o'er Cupid's flower
Lewis and Short avoiding sport
turn over

Oh Latona's daughter/of greatest (masculine)/
great (feminine)/progeny of Jove
whom mother/by the/pertaining to Delos/
bore (gave birth to)/olive tree

To make you mistress of the peaks
the green retreats
secret paths
laughing streams

You the virgin in the moonlight
patroness of labour pains
you the empress of the crossways
'Moon Mask' your embroidered name-tape

You presiding over sick bay's
blanketed heaps with menstrual cramps
setting rhythms that will bring un-
wasted eggs to harvest festival

Holy by what name you choose
hover as we seek to gloss
the gerund in the haunted hatband's
Serviendo crescimus[2]

---

2   'In service we grow', the motto of Woking Girls' Grammar
    School

35

Whisper papyrus rope
Slow draw down exhale
A spell over hollow bamboo
Make him follow me

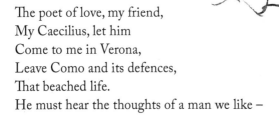

The poet of love, my friend,
My Caecilius, let him
Come to me in Verona,
Leave Como and its defences,
That beached life.
He must hear the thoughts of a man we like –

If he's wise he'll scorch right up the track
Even if some blanched female
Tries to drag him back,
Twines her tentacles
Around him, maddened by
Her eggs, begs him to stay.

The grapevine says
There's one already
Ripe to die from disappointed love:
Now she's read his draft
About the goddess mother
She's a bitch on heat.

Girl, I sympathise. You're
Closer to the edge than Sappho's muse:
'Incomplete Approach to the Insistent
Ovulator' by Caecilius –
Got to admire him.

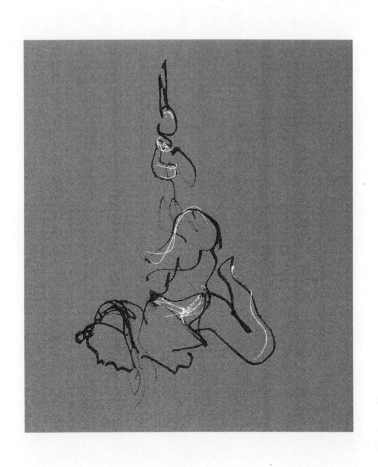

36

Now we turn to the Andrex annals
Scribbled by Mr Voluble –
They'll let Mistress keep her promise
To Venus and Cupid, no less.

She swears on her high-gloss pile of Taschen books
That if I come back to her bonds
And don't spike her on spondees
She'll take the juiciest chunks
By the worst poet and let the fire-god Vulcan
(How appropriate, he's lame) scorch them
In her Stefano Ferrara pizza oven.
The world's worst woman thinks it's some kind of
Joke about my selected works.

Let Venus (emerging from the pool to drip
Blessings on Araki's collectors' editions
While noting a personal preference for Sugiura)
Stamp a receipt for a smart substitution:

Here's Mr Voluble's epic crap –
Into the flames, a shoddy shitfest.

37

You boys queueing outside Berlin Berlin –
You think you're the only ones with cocks,
Let in to fuck the girls
While the rest of us get herded away?
Have another think.

*The poet fantasises about ejaculating in the reluctant faces of two
hundred male clubbers. He then considers his options.*

I'll squirt correctly spelt obscene graffiti
All over your façade

Because the girl who broke out of my hold –
Loved with more love
Than other women will reap,
The one I had such brutal fights to keep –
Is your house dominant.

They all want her, the cream of the alphas and –
Harder for me to bear – the bottom feeders

Especially you, lord of the hairy-arsed,
All the way from Saragossa's
Plague-zone of randy fluffy bunnies –
Señor Egnatius, raised to foreign nobility
By your clogged beard and glaring expat teeth
Scrubbed with vintage Spanish urine.

The poet puts down his tools and goes for a pee.

38

… with a murmur… my ravings…

Can't go on but does
Can't be borne but must be
Down and the weight bears down
Each day each hour Cornificius[3]
Bad for your Catullus
But have you written the least
The tiniest scrap to calm me?
Feel my rage. Is this all your love means?

Whisper me a consolation please
Sadder than Housman's trembling tears

---

3   This might be Quintus Cornificius, poet and military
    commander, who left one fragment of poetry:
    deducta mihi voce garrienti
    subdued/(to?) me/voice/chattering

39

Egnatius, what bright teeth you have!
All the better to dazzle a lighthouse, dear.

If some poor sod is in the dock and counsel's
Pumping out the jury's tear ducts – gleam!
If a mother's sobbing at the grave
Of her devoted only son – say cheese!
Wherever, whatever, always on full beam.
His social morbidity is unacceptable.

Stop doing all that glistening and listen,
Egnatius. If you were premier arrondissement
Material, or from the shires, the home counties,
The fens, even just north of the park like me
Or anywhere else with proper dental hygiene,
I'd still deplore you baring that glaring enamel:
Stupid grins should be punched out on principle.

Your problem is, you're from that place we don't
Mention – the Hispanic provinces,
Where the locals freshen teeth and sore gums
With their warm piss – the sparklier your smile,
The bigger your morning hit of uric acid.

40

Mr Grey, what slip of the mind
Drove a creature like you
Into my lines?

Did you rub a genie's lamp
And wake up in this stupid fight?

You want to be talked about in the vernacular
Whatever the damage?

You will be.
You got too close to Mistress.
The term is life.

41

Ameana, Lady Fuck-me,
Tried to bill me for 10k –
That one with the fretwork septum
And the bankrupt beach-bum ponce.

What did Jimmy Goldsmith say?
'Beauty is a social necessity.'

Gather round and get her sectioned –
Show her what a cheap brass looks like.

42

I'll chuck verbiage at her,
Give it the works.
That fat slag thinks I'm a joke
And won't return my poetry notebook. Imagine!

Let's go after her and get it back.
Which one? That specimen
Waddling along with her amdram laugh.

Butcher's-dog-faced bitch. Block her path.
'Fat slag, give back his notebook!
Give him back his Moleskine, you fat slag!'

She doesn't give a toss, the dirty cow.
[Put something filthy here/leave a space]

Don't give up.
At least we'll rub her dogface in it.

So, louder:
'Fat slag, we said Moleskine, not foreskin.
Give it back, you fat slag!'

Still nothing. We'll change tactics
And get a result this time:

'Mother Superior – *s'il vous plaît* – the works?'

43

And a big Veronese hello to you, lady.
You could fix your nose hammer toes eyebags nails
Oral hygiene
Even if your tongue stays unpegged
And the bankrupt beachboy's a fixture

But back home they say you don't need any work done –
That you're Mistress's equal
[Shudders]

44

Dear family farm – and tell those postcode fetishists
You're in the sticks but satisfy the trend police –
I fled to your neat villa with my ravaged lungs,
Self-inflicted as I overdid the trough
Chez Sestius, where I had to read his gastric-flu-
Inducing rants against some hapless candidate –

I came to you a shivering bronchitic mess
And found a cure in sleep and nettle soup. Next time
I'll let his toxic ramblings ravage him, not me.
Bile's on the menu when he writes RSVP.

*The thee and thou and thy of the original
Got lost on the wrong side of the North Orbital*

Metre: scazon

45

Septimius perched his girlfriend Acme
On his knee. 'Poppet,' he said,
'If I'm not properly prepared
To pine for you with desperate love,
Panting in perpetuity,
Then chop me up with pickled peppers,
Make me into vindaloo
And feed me to the lions.'

Someone dressed as Cupid did a line
From left to right and sneezed but that was fine.

Acme lightly raised her head,
Kissed her lover's pooling eyes
With scarlet lips and said, 'My darling
Septimillus, we'll stay bound
In just one service, and I'll feel it
More than you because you'll seal it
On my skin with melted wax.'

Cupid passed the kutchie on the left hand
Side and sneezed – a good omen. Bless you.

Now with coupledom's gold card,
Watch these padlocked lovebirds preening.
Poor Septimius chooses Acme,
Turns down postings (Syria, Britain).
Fixed on her Septimius,
Acme's rewarded with good kinky sex.

Who could challenge for their gleaming
His-and-hers trophy in the Venus stakes?

Cupid and my Campaspe play'd
At cards for kisses

I could have stopped there
You were the best kisser
Never needed to progress
Beyond the kissing
Only the kissing
Your soft mouth for hours forever
So stick that on your gilt-framed reproduction

But now the cherry hung with snow
Has been cut down so I must go.
I won't give a sparrow's fart
For Housman's guilt or Cupid's dart

And you'll be my Echo without knowing
I'll be closer than your gilt-flecked frosted lipstick
Kissing your words
In a scatter of sweet coloured hundreds and thousands

Carry me across the lands and waters
For this sad rite
Hail, mortal. Hail!
So, goodnight

References to Britain and Syria suggest that this poem might have
been written towards the end of Catullus's life.

Cupid and my Campaspe play'd/At cards for kisses
begins a poem by John Lyly (1553–1606).

A.E. Housman wrote:

About the woodlands I will go/To see the cherry hung with snow.

The last two lines of this version are fairy words from *A Midsummer Night's Dream*.

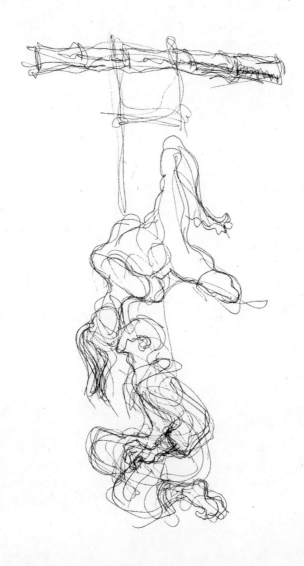

46

Sprung from shielding by a sigh on skin…

Pent-up stormy skies at the equinox are
Calmed by breath of a traveller's west wind.
You can leave the plains of duty, Catullus,
And the stuffy trap of productivity:
Book a one-way seat to city glitter,
Let your blanched ambition find the light,
Map the spaces where you'll dance and run.

Friends so close without touch in this ordeal – we've
Come too far from our intended roads, let's
Part and meet our freedom in scattered ways.

'Shielding' has come to mean 'staying at home for health reasons during a pandemic'.

47

Pig. And your pig-pen friend
The Socrates wannabe –
Piso's twin left hands
Spreading virus and famine,
Nowhere out of bounds.

Did that worn-out prick
Slip you extra rations
Ahead of my own pets
Veranius and Fabullus?
You graze between meals on his massive
Stockpile while my boys
Slink to the foodbank

48

Let me do that
Japanese thing
Juventius
Lick your eyeball
Saliva saline
Oculus
Osculation
Ooh your big
Round O eyes
No zeros
Haven't got those
I'm kissing you
A million times better
One two three
Pass it to me
This one has lots of
Little dry seeds look
Do they pop
Never stop

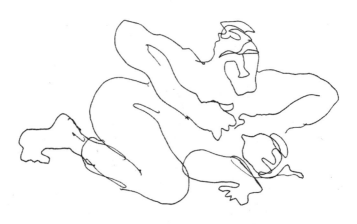

49

Rome's present, past and future time will show
No one does rhetoric like you, Cicero.
Catullus sends you thanks, his very best.

Of all the poets, he's the very worst –
That is, as much the worst at making sense
As you are the best counsel for defence.
Lol had you there pal.

50

Yesterday we filled
A void, Licinius...

Coils to lines on skin
Coining words for torso
Torment torque torsion
Flipped the Master switch
Who'll be Torquemada?
Purple and white hide
Jute-burned scored
Red at the denouement

Now alone in the night
Too full of you to eat
No sleep to smother fires
Squirming churning the covers
Spreadeagled aching for daylight
Muscles sore nerves
Numb from the tourniquet
I will open out the book of you
Make you soar with eagles over the edge

So be meek my love and take the hurt
Which Nemesis spears through me.
She's ruthless. Don't talk back.

51

I can't compete with the rock-god superhero
God's begging him to accept the shiniest halo
That man intent on you
Ogling provoking

Your sexy laughter I'm muted
My nerves torn out with hooks
Because when I see you Clodia I
Fumble for a line and

<*Find a lacuna*>

Mouth crammed with earth
Limbs hot and clumsy with longing
High tide pounding my skull
Trashed headlights and a windscreen
Crazed to opacity

Idling Catullus it stalls your intention
And maidens call it love-in-idleness
Without a plan you're restless and distracted
Idle coasting toppled kings and golden
Cities in legends

There is a line missing from the original, where shown in hairpins. Catullus's first three stanzas are a translation of Sappho 31. This last stanza quotes Oberon in *A Midsummer Night's Dream*.

51

Oh go ahead with giving head to the godhead
God help us he outdogs the gods of dogging
Monopolising you with his cheap tactics
Paying attention

Making you laugh and my receptors go haywire
Because one look at you Mistress and
I can't even form a polite request
For *semenawa*

My tongue dries cold blue tied to bamboo
Slung body hurts in tight jute knots
Rope burns and bare skin flinches from hot wax drips
Techno rattles my brain
Stinging eyes
Submit to the blindfold and and

Wanking, Orlando. It's unproductive.
Wanking makes you fretful and distracted.
Legendary kings and shiny cities,
Lost to wanking.

52

Still here, Catullus? Why put off the lethal dose?
Lies and cruelty are the only cards in play
With maniacs in charge and Armageddon close.
Don't hang around, Catullus. Here's the tourniquet.

Metre: scazon

53

Laughter in court
When my Calvus
(Not very tall)
Finished throwing the book at Vatinius –

Someone raised his hands to heaven in awe
And said, 'That runty cunt's convincing!'

Or if you like puns
He said, 'That short-arse likes long sentences!'

Well it broke the tension.
You had to be there
And even if you weren't
You needed to look average,

Not stand out.

54

Dead on arrival

What's the point?
If you can't decipher it
Through your time-travel telescope,
Here's a thought:
Don't bother.

So, Otho, God knows who he is,
Well his head, or his actual dick head,
Is little or weak,

Then some mystery wordlet –
Maybe Hirrus, look him up
If you're here for the critical craic

And I could be haranguing a yokel
(Rustic**e**, rhymes with Caesar, J.)
Or if you read rustic**a**
(Rhymes with CaesAR)
That describes the dirt-streaked legs.

Here's another unknown, might be
Lucius Scribonius Libo, like I care –
Still, I analyse his farts for anyone interested
Which I can see you're not

But I'll be overjoyed if the above
Upsets a Certain Person
Along with some old guy called Sufficius or Fufidius –
I tell you, he'll need more than cryogenics

< Textual loss here, you won't find it, peasants>

         you'll throw another tantrum
Drenched by my water pistol poetry squirt,
Oh Great Chief Somebody I want to hurt.

Next time the engine loses power
Remember what your parachute's for.

55

All right, I'll beg.
Have pity.
Where's your bolt-hole?

I've scoured the Admiral Duncan, The George and Dragon,
The Royal Vauxhall Tavern and Senate House Library.

I pounced on a ladyboy act at Duckie
Although their make-up masks looked innocent:
'Hand over Camerius, you degenerate slags.'
One whipped out a credible fake pair:
'Here he is, mate, hiding in my bra.'

I might as well be seeking The Coleherne
Or the Pillars of Hercules long closed down,
Such is the cruelty of your absence, my dear.

So, where?
And are you here or there?
I mean, do you have sex with girls now, white ones?

Talk. But if you keep your mouth clenched shut
You'll throw away the peak rewards of love.
Venus likes a full confessional

Or if you like, don't make a sound,
Just as long as I can join your harem.

56

Oh you'll love this
Bloody hilarious
Cato yes no really look at me
Don't go
Too funny
So I take some G
Sneak into the dungeon
On my own
Find a kid
Pounding some girl
I don't bother to ask
(So slap my wrist
It's a stupid rule anyway)
And make him the meat in the sandwich

Look, am I boring you or something
I bored him with this skewer lol
OK you can read it another way
It's dark and I'm dead
There was no girl
Only Mistress's boy slave

Or her brother

Beating time to thoughts of her as we do
Oh Christ look have some of this
Of course I can handle it

Alternative readings make the event obscure so I offer three versions.

57

Twin offenders, greedy benders,
Mister Marble Balls and Caesar,
Bookended rotten borough buggers
(*Quelle surprise*, they're packed with drug-
Resistant STDs picked up
On city prowls or seafront trawls),
Arse-parsing their two-in-a-gondola
Intellectual pseudocracy,
Equally bent on adultery,
Competitive group sex with under-age
Girls a speciality.

Star turn, four hands one keyboard.

58

Glue. Bit.

Oh Caelius –

Mistress, Herself, her Worship, our own Lady of the
Labia, the one the poet loved
More than himself and all the rest –

Now downloadable dogging in urban areas
And choking on locally elected members

58 (B)

Not even if I hurtled through the spaceways
Or nailed the mile at three minutes forty-two
Or hailed a drone taxi with a thermal sensor
Or rode a feather-hoofed police horse cruising
At supersonic speed – harness me a
Matching pair of greys, Camerius –
No, the quest would leave me bone-tired and wasted,
My dear, before I found and made you fast.

59

That redhead raised on Bologna sausage
Goes down on Harry. She's married to some toff.
You've often filmed her in the cemetery car park –
She'll grab the hot scraps, lunge for
A mouthful rearing out of restraint
While the stubbly embalmer bangs away at her.

60

You got your manners from scavenging mountain lions?
Or self-aborted from the foul prolapsed
Uterus of

Scylla the howling dog-
Lover? Is that why you despise
A beggar's plea of urgent need?
Go down. To hell. Your heat, your heart of a bitch.

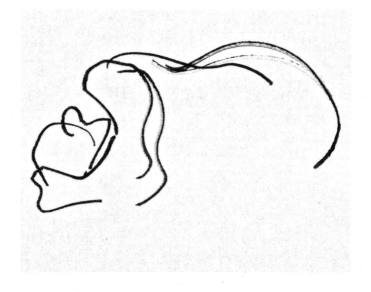

6 1

*'The bride and groom are ideally suited to each other and I should
know because I've had them both.'*

Best man's speech, England, 1970s

Oh! Son of bless'd Urania
(Mistress of the mushroom cloud),
Fall into a cab in Soho –
It's your job to haul a fainting
Virgin down the aisle. We call you
Hymenaeus.

Drag up like the bride, be happy,
Wind sweet marijuana, sorry,
Marjoram in your tiara,
Wear a veil shot with gold lamé,
Your stilettos a stab of citrus
Over your cricket socks.

It's a good day to get high,
Blast out hymns in your falsetto,
Stamp and twirl your pinewood torch –

Our Junia is going to marry
Manlius, like Venus awaiting
Judgement in the beauty contest,
Virgin a hot tip to win,
Clutching her sparkly myrtle posy,
Pure white flowers sprayed with dew
By dryads to keep themselves amused.

Leave the nymphets where you found them
In that bar for out-of-work actors.
Ask the new mistress of the house to
Head for the playroom and express
Her desire for her new husband
Bound in ropes as tight as ivy
Embracing a trunk.

Virgin bridesmaids, we'll be warbling
Love divine, all loves excelling
When your day comes, but for now
Sing the hymen chorus, make him
Scramble into best-man mode.
Let's big up his self-importance:

Hymenaeus, top of the gods
For dynasty-fixated parents,
Undressed brides and fumbling grooms –
You pull an adolescent girl
From Mummy's arms and hand her to
A gawky boy, oh clever
Hymenaeus.

Venus's wholesome look
Would melt in sleaze without you

No home guarantees
Legitimate heirs without you

There's no sure supply
Of border guards without you

You're a smart god, Hymenaeus

Slide the bolt open, girl, come out.
Watch the burning torches flare
Like comet tails

<*loss*>

      learnt inhibition
Makes her falter. As the din
Encroaches – is it human? – she's in
Tears because it's time to go.

Pack those tears away, Auruncu-
leia. You won't be outshone:
A prettier face won't catch the sun
Today.

You're our slender wild white Roman
Hyacinth who makes the rich
Collector's flowers look garish with
Her grace… Now move it please or you'll be
Late.

Here comes the bride. *O, she doth teach*
The torches to burn bright!

No, he really isn't seeing
Other women on the quiet.
He's a tit man and you've got
The gear to tempt him home at night.
Here's a tip, he's a submissive –
Learn some simple bondage ties,
A bit of role play, he'll be happy.

Oh! Bed – on which the town bicycle

from the ivory leg of the couch.
I trust I've made that clear. The boss

Will revel in it. Sexy nights
Of fantasy fulfilment. Plenty
More at lunchtime. Hurry up, child,
Haven't got all day.
OK choirboys, hoist your torches,
Goldilocks is on her way,
Don't sound ragged, here's an A:

All things bright and beautiful
Rhyme and hymen and unreason,
Welcome to the wedding season.

That? Oh he's the groom's ex-boyfriend,
Chucking walnuts at the pageboys.
It's a custom hereabouts.

Oi, you lazy little sod,
What are those nuts for? You've fiddled
With them long enough, now find
Another randy sugar daddy.
Low-grade MILFs disgust you but
We no longer find you cute
Now your beard is coming out.
Watch that bag of nuts, kid.

Word is, bridegroom – too much aftershave –
You don't want to give up schoolboys,
But they're for us bachelors.
Now you'll have to do without.
Don't blame me, blame Hymenaeus.

Lady, keep your legs uncrossed
Or he'll look for it elsewhere.
It's a nice house in a classy
Postcode, be content with that
Until your white-haired tremor makes you
Nod agreement willy-nilly.
Don't thank me, thank Hymenaeus.

Over the threshold with you and your
Tippy-toe golden shoes, it's lucky,
Through the high-gloss entrance. Bridegroom's
Resting on the wine-dark couch, as
Motivated as his spouse –
It's just less obvious at the moment.
Hymenaeus will fix all that.

Pageboy in your sawn-off tux,
Release the girl-bride's dainty little
Arm: she'll totter to the bed.
Ladies saddled with old husbands,
Put this sweetheart in position.

Man, she's ready in your master suite.
You know, she's really quite –

Dazzling little face
Coming into bloom
Daisy petal white
Silky poppy gold…

Of course. You're heaven to look at too,
Venus herself would fancy you.
Get on with it.

Yes, good old goddess, she'll help out
Now your desire is palpable.
Can you count the stars that brightly
Twinkle in the midnight sky
Or grains of sand in the Sahara.
Whatever. That's to enumerate
Your vanilla sex games. You'll go for
Quantity, not quality –
Don't tell me, I'm bored already.

Keep the lineage on track.
Let me see a micro-Manlius
Wriggling on his mummy's knee,
Pointing with chubby fingers,
Gurgling at daddy.

Pray he looks like just like his father
So that facial recognition
Verifies his mother's conduct.
Just as well the son of Odysseus
Didn't take after Penelope.
Imagine.

Thank you bridesmaids, close the door.
Well that was fun.
Newlyweds, have a good life
On the reproductive treadmill –
All there is for shackled couples
At your age.
Now, who'd like another drink?

62

Vespas vespers passeggiata
Vespertinal bell

Vespertilio *Latin for bat (the mammal)*
Vesta Tilley male impersonator

Vesta goddess of the hearth
Vestal Virgins keepers of the flame
Swan Vestas matches made of aspen

'I trembling like an aspen leaf stood sad and bloodlesse quyght.'[4]

Boys:
Starry pinpricks in the dusk
Before our big pricks turn to dust
Time to leave the well-stocked bar
Virgo's high and on her way
Let her hear the wedding chant
That hymen better be real, girl, not from a bow-tied Wimpole
Street abortionist.

Girls:
Watch the boys. They've made their move.
Get in place, mark your opponent
Under artificial light.
Look how confident they are –
Bunch of Eurovision winners.
Absence of what some people imagine a hymen might be like has
led to assault, imprisonment, murder and suicide.

---

4   Arthur Golding, *Metamorphoses* XIV line 245

Boys:
Guys, this isn't in the bag.
Look – that's what you call rehearsing.
They've got focus. We're a mess.
At this rate they deserve to win
So concentrate and mark your woman.
Some girls are born without a noticeable hymen.

Girls:
Evening star, the most sadistic
Searchlight in the sky: you gouge
The daughter from her mother's arms,
Daughter clinging to her mother,
Hand her to some randy lout
Like a general when he's seized the state.
*The causes of bleeding in the female are ignorance and clumsiness in
the male.*

Boys:
Evening star, you shed light on the
Case and ratify the deed
Signed by parents then by husbands.
It's enacted when you rise:
Heaven sets the time to close.
Virginity tests are legal in many jurisdictions. They are unscientific.

Girls:
The evening star has abducted our sister

<*loss*>

Boys:
Then you switch to night security.
Burglars sneak out in the dark
But you apprehend them when you
Flood the sky at dawn. Females
Complain about their bedtime duty
But you know they want it really.
Virginity kits are sold online. Ancients used blood in a fish bladder.

Girls:
In the cloistered garden is a
Secret flower, safe from flocks and
Ploughshares, stroked by air and nursed by
Sunlight, fed by rain – the crux of
Stifled longing for boys and girls.
When a sharp nail nips the stalk
No one wants the fallen petals.
Virgin state is loved by all
But if purity is spoiled
Boys lose interest, girls grow cold.
A bride may file a fingernail to a point and cut her thigh so that she bleeds on to the sheet which must be exhibited to her family.

Boys:
Vine neglected on bare field
Never has a ripened yield.
Single state is unforgiving,
Main stem flops and furthest striving
Tendril barely reaches root:
Farmer and beast squash underfoot.

Vine submits to husbandry –
Farmer digs and beast comes by.
If she's not correctly mated
She grows old uncultivated.
Bound to elm tree's rising trunk
She is money in the bank
Earning interest on her man's respect,
Not a millstone round her father's neck.

Don't go fighting marriage wars
Girl. Your body isn't yours.
One third is assigned to father,
One more third allowed to mother.
What's left over is for you
Making one share against two.
During the service they transfer
Theirs to the groom so call him sir.
'Honour, high honour and renown,
To Hymen, god of every town!'[5]

Poem 62 emerged in the ninth century as the only surviving work by
Catullus until this collection was found c1300.

---

5   Shakespeare, *As You Like It*

63

Attis

Superhighway vector Otis otorhinolaryngeal
Sea spray dream snow yacht lane ketamised to Anatolia

Skimming deep realities Attis scudded over water
Pierced the sunless forest rimming the home of the goddess
  mother
Crested a personal best of disgust mind undone
Sawed into his scrotal sac with sharp serrated stone
Felt the tag of maleness gone
Warm blood spattered on the ground
Grasped taut skin
With snowdrift hands

Your own tympanum mother and your labyrinth beyond

Pattered out a rhythm on the scraped bull's hide
And set off in the feminine
To quaver at her copyists:

'Reach for the porcelain shepherdess
On your mother's high pine shelf.
You follow my traces
Like displaced flocks
Seeking new folds in untranslated landscapes.
The sea tried to drown you in salt-eroded wrecks,
You gelded yourselves in disgust at grown-up sex –
Now make your exile fodder to amuse
Our Mistress of Dindymus and the Epididymis.

Run to her woods
Where tinnitus screeches,
The tympanum booms,
Hollow bones groan,
Hair-thrashing fangirls
Are roped with ivy
And worshippers scream
In ritual convulsions.

There in the name of the goddess her acolytes levitate –
We'll set the pace with the quickstep and Viennese waltz.'

Travesty-Attis
Reached a lacuna.
The choir of transcribers
Growled and trilled,
The tympanum buzzed,
Tinnitus whistled,
Annotators
Made for the groves.

Confused and panting like a
Recalcitrant bride, Attis
Struggled to lead the chorus
Crashing through the dark texts.
Weary they crawled at last
Into the mother's refuge.
Soothed by a tender stupor
They fell asleep without supper.

When the sun's barefaced searchlight
Purged the blank sky,
The hard ground, the harsh sea
And banished soporifics with thundering headaches,

The sleep god prodded Attis awake
And scurried off to the arms of his anxious wife.

After a night of release from bad dreams,
Bitter recall drove Attis sobbing
Back to the amniotic sea of vastness.

'Oh Mummy, oh my first home, where I was safe,
I'm so unhappy.
I ran away, as wretched as fugitive slaves,
And found the white powder mountain
Where terror crouches in frozen dens.
Mania dragged me to each dark hiding place
But Mummy I can't find you here.
I long to hold you in my gaze
For this one flicker of sanity.

Must I be cast out, give up possessions,
People who love me, places where I shine?
The clubs, the pool, the park for five-a-side?
I can't bear the pain on pain.
Is there a human part I haven't played?
Woman, man, hormonal adolescent,
Child. They eyed me at the gym, with my oiled
Torso. I had all the followers.
Every morning I woke up to streams
Of hearts and likes.
Am I now the goddess mother's full-time
Slave but just half man?

Am I washed up on a green waste
Under the jagged peaks of the frigid mountain,
Alone with the hart and the hog in the wood and the forest?
Now what I did stabs home.
Now I am punished.'

Spiralling from scarlet lips, this lament
Coiled along the goddess mother's cochleae.
She raised the yoke from her twin carriage
Dragons and flicked the nearside predator:

'Hound him back to madness and the forest
For daring to resist my domination.
Use your barbed tail for self-flagellation.
Burst eardrums. Snort red fire.' The queen of spite
Let go. The frantic monster lashed its hide,
Roared and hurtled across the smouldering scrub
To bleached wet sands where Attis stood forlorn
On the amniotic fluid's glaring
Brink, *lŏcă lītŏrĭs*.

The dragon lunged, the manic creature plunged
Back into the scene, a submissive forever.

Goddess mother, supervisor, bitch –
Keep me free from all this lunacy, Mistress.
Let the others overdose and switch.
What I mean is, can I call you Mummy?
She called me Darling.

64

Stick or twist

And did you see Swinburne presiding
At The Pines, Putney Hill, in a trance
Of song and the sea, coinciding
With The Pirates of Penzance?
The river nearby carried oarsmen
And dolorous thoughts of romance
While 'the pain that is all but a pleasure
Will change for the pleasure that's all
But pain' wrote W.S. Gilbert,
Shooting Oscar a glance. [6]

Stumpwork:
High-born pines
Pitched down Mount Pelion,
Splashed in the clear Aegean and swam east
When the fresh Greek crop of hard men
Braved the long ship's maiden voyage
Skimming the lapis salt expanse
With firwood oars
To liberate the golden fleece from barbarians
Given the full consent of its owner the ram
Who also agreed to be bred for sacrifice.

---

6   In 1879 Algernon Charles Swinburne moved into The Pines
     (pineapples in this case), and *The Pirates of Penzance; or, The
     Slave of Duty* (by Gilbert and Sullivan) was first performed.
     The stanza includes references to Swinburne's *Dolores* and *To
     Catullus*. The quotation is from Gilbert's comic opera *Patience*.

Crafted by the goddess who patrolled
The Greeks' moral high ground,
Argo flew at a hint of breath,
Curved hull corseted with woven pine,
And scored a rudimentary shipping lane
On the unmarked bloom of Neptune's wife.

As her prow incised the windswept seascape
And oar-power flicked the coiled waves to meringue,
Glistening faces peered out of the turmoil:
For the rest of their lives the mortal crew
Would say they saw all fifty Nereids rise open-
Mouthed at the floating revelation, naked
As far as the remembered breasts of my wet nurse
Streaked with opaque pearlescence

Then Peleus (human) was convulsed with love
For Thetis (sea-nymph), much to the joy of the gene-pool.
Thetis thought it smart to marry out
And Father Jupiter, for all his thunder,
Wouldn't put them asunder.

Oh! If we could choose our time
The lost is best –
An age of gorgeous gods and godlike others
With glamorous mothers
When sex made better people
Before we edged each other to extinction

<*loss*>

But I will summon you for a song at least
And Peleus, you above the rest,
Higher than your wedding torches'

Toxic emissions.
You are Thessaly's banker –
Jupiter himself deposits love –

And you make headlines. Has the longed-for beauty
Thetis picked you out? Her grandparents
Franchise the sea – will they allow it?
Come the day,
The whole of Thessaly, clutching invitations,
Flocks to the palace to ogle, spilling glee,
Brandishing presents, abandoning production –

Bullocks' necks grow soft
Unyoked, no sprawling vine
Is weeded with a drag hoe
Let me be your drag ho,
No sharp iron is ox-
Drawn to gouge a furrow,
No tree's chilling shade
Pruned hard back with metal,
Rust of brute neglect
Makes the ploughshare brittle

While the Bidden City glares with bullion.
Ivory inlay winks and twinkles in thrones
Generously sponsored by the elephants,
Gleaming goblets beam along the tables,
Royal treasure revels in refraction.
At the heart, a marriage bed that glints
With Indian tusks (see above), awaits the goddess.
Its coverlet has a ground of smouldering heliotrope
Fast-dyed with the help of purpling sea-snails
Who offer up themselves in industrial quantity.
Panels of embroidered people in stories

Use the soft outsides of animals,
Vegetable threads and dyes, and lustrous
Wiry filaments of silver-gilt
To illuminate heroic legends
With ancient skill that we can only wonder at.

This one shows the first person who left me –
Hold a whorled shell to your ear for the soundtrack,
The rhythm of waves on the white sands of Naxos.

Theseus (or, The Slave of Duty) and
His crew cast off in haste.
Feral anguish of rejection
Grips Ariadne, gazing, glazed, bewildered,
Waking from a dream of marble halls

To find myself abandoned on the shore
While you with your out-of-office head
Row hard and fling your broken promises
Into the high winds.
Stranded sad-eyed with the bladderwrack
I stare, a dusted alabaster maenad.
Grief breaks over me.
This silly filmy slip
You thought such a great idea
With platinum Marilyn hair
Performs its loose-strap slither down my shaved
Torso, pooling where the lacy water
Seethes around my varnished toe-nails.
Heedless of the flimsy floating drag
I fix my heart and fractured thought on
You, Theseus. Oh, my wretched girl-mind,
How thoroughly Aphrodite drove me out of it,
Sowing thorny tortures in my soul when

Theseus read the small print, grew defiant,
Left the scimitar shoreline of Piraeus
To throw the textbook at an unfair foreign
Jurisdiction,
All the jargon,
Keen to void
Oppressive contract
Terms. His father,
King of Athens
(Coerced by plague),
Said yes to blood fee
When a Cretan prince – Ariadne's brother –
Fetched up dead on Athenian turf. The deal:
A regular haul of perfect male and female
Virgins shipped across as ambient snacks
For the King of Crete's voracious stepson,
The man-bull Minotaur held underground.

Pained by the narrowness of force majeure
And for love of Athens,
Theseus put his own life on the table
In place of human cattle.
Fair winds and an agile craft carried him
To face down the magnificence and intellect
Of Minos.

        Ariadne – all her longings
Hot-housed in the palace,
Fostered by sugary fangirl fantasies
Bred in her single bed, knowing
Security in Mummy's cuddle,
Spraying on Candy Kiss and Angel,
Playing with lilac blusher and primrose lipstick –

Turned to the stranger
And stared.
The lenses of her hungry eyes
Magnified the spark
And lit a flare of agonised desire.

Callous Cupid, holy delinquent
Loading human joy with pain,
And Venus, on your casual rounds –
Both of you wasters, burning up your girl toy
Set alight by that blond poster boy.

Her heart clattering a false rhythm of fear,
She grew paler than marsh light caught on gold
When Theseus went to jump the irresistible
Monster, eat or be eaten, take, be taken.
She mouthed her furtive promises to gods –
Unripe offerings, but they struck home.

Imagining a Taurus Mountains scene
Where bulldozed oaks and conifers oozing resin
Tip and topple,
Take on painful torsions, make giant crush patterns,
Theseus went neither left nor right
But straight and low,
Saw the monster as an entrance,
Not an exit,
Made the bull-form switch, submit,
Offer up its skin as charmed as snakes,
Be hurt, spun, translated, floored, powered down.

Theseus walked back alone,
Let the rope trail solve the mystery
And took the credit safely past blind alleys:
Shouts of praise rang in his bony labyrinth.

To pick up threads –
Daughter shrinks from Daddy's eye,
Shrugs off sister and Mummy rictus-smiling
For her child's wretched sake –
They won't understand her boy crush outranks them –
He abducts her to island,
They 'marry',
She falls asleep,
He abandons 'wife', she opens her eyes,

Panics, wails,
Scales broken cliffs
To scour the agitated naked horizon,
Tucks up her diaphanous skirt
(Keeping it dry, but why not say
Her legs are bare for the relentless cold
Eye), greets breakers pushing her away,

Weeps into chilly air,
Bleats out the last notes of her mortal despair:

You made me elope for this, you bastard?
Leave my home and family to be dumped?
Did you read it in your player's manual?
'Ignore their sob stuff about the way to behave.
They put out for the Mister Darcy bullshit
So do what you want then clear off home.'
I didn't hear any of that in your whiny pleading
But promises of happy married life
Flew like confetti in a hurricane.

Never trust a lover
Made from air and water
With your breakable parts.
If you give your heart
The deal becomes about
What's hard and where's a hole.
Promises are wild:
As the kettle boils
Steam becomes the driver
But when urges cool,
Forever ices over:
All those things he swore
Scroll out on the wind
And the frozen river.

When you fell from that
Expensive permanent high,
Spoilt aristo boy,
My trick got you out
And when my back was turned my brother died.
I stayed on but you lied and lied and lied.

I thought you needed me.
Now you've left me prey,
Just so much raw meat
For fang and claw and beak,
No ritual hand to scatter
Earth on my hope's rifled bones.

And when I cried for my wet nurse, my hot tears
Trickled into the crevices of my ears.

As for your mother,
Some jealous feral man-eater short on love,
Or was she ambiguous
Like you, amphibian,
Fouling the sea-bed,
Spawning in furious waves
That spat you out on shore?
And bullies father bullies
But if your fear of his old-school
Punishment ruled out
Our open travesty,
You could at least have led me
Home in fetters as your
Helpless house-slave, cooling
The soles of Master's feet
With kisses and clear water,
Stroking the rumpled purple
Cover on your bed
Smooth again. Now sleeps
The crimson petal, now
The white, Sir.

But what's the point of talking at the air?
It doesn't care.

He's half a sea away.
There's nothing human in the washed-up weed,
Just nature's cruelty.
This is a prison cell turned inside-out.

What do they say in CBT? Make a list.

1. Call back time

    a) Athenians couldn't find Crete on the map
    b) there was no tribute of virgins
    c) the bull was a pushover
    d) we didn't have the handsome prince to stay
    e) we did but he was sweet, not all deceit

2. Find hope/help

    a) Crete (home) but dangerous voyage
    b) Daddy
        i)   in Crete
        ii) my bull-brother's blood spattered...
    c) ...my loving so-called husband. Who changed
        course.

I'm marooned on a barren bedspread.

Shelter – tent stitch, trellis stitch
First aid – blanket stitch
Water – wave stitch
Food – scallop stitch, oyster stitch, snail's trail
Escape – ladder stitch, running stitch, fly stitch
Dreams – knotted Cretan, crewel work, whip stitch

And death is sewing me a shroud
But I won't come undone in the dark

Before I vent my teenage spite in prayer.
I'll die of what you did.
Let gods judge what's fair.
Mine will make you pay.

Eumenides, your wigs of swirling snakes
Hiss like the acid slewing out of your mouths.
Now come down to me.
I am liquid fire.
Obsession made me a slave.
Let my hatred live.
Theseus broke his promise and broke me.
Make him wreck himself and what he touches.

Beached girl prayed
With wounded heart,
Begged that pain
Be passed on.
Father ruling
Earth and sky
Nodded, causing
Sea-quake, star-shake
So that Theseus
Scanning charts
Failed to notice
Swirls of absent-
Mindedness
And forgot
To raise that sign
In sight of port
Which would have shown
His anguished father
That he was alive.

Backstitch:
As Theseus was leaving
Safe harbour at Athens
His father Aegeus embraced him,
Banking on the sea-winds:

'You are my only son –
Long life means less than that.
You came to me so late.
I'm forced to let you play
With death when mine is close.
My bad luck and your
Implacable sense of right
Carry you away

Before my failing eyes
Can catch your cherished image.
No thin cheers from me,
And don't fly good luck signals.
I'll perform grievance – watch me
Scour my white-haired scalp
With Earth and dust to defile it.
Now, hang dyed canvas from your mast at sea.
Indigo will tell the burnt-out story
Of my bereavement
But just in case Athena's grace ordains
A jet of blood from the beast to play on your hand,
Keep this sharp in your memory –
Don't let your misty vagueness rub it out:
When you see our hills, lower the mourning,
Hoist the sun-bleached sails with braided sheets
And I'll be in a frenzy of relief
To know you're safe.'

Theseus tried to remember until he didn't.
These orders parted like so many clouds
Shooed from snowy peaks by gusty winds.
Aegeus, peering from the Acropolis,
Old eyes blurred with anxious tears,
Saw inky bellying sails and jumped
Headlong from the summit, thinking
Fate's machine had mangled Theseus –
Who walked into his father's stricken house
Still proud but shouldering a weight of grief
To balance what he'd casually inflicted
On poor Ariadne as, half-dressed, miserable,
She watched his ship diminish and battered her wings
Against the dead ends of her labyrinth

That you loved me still the same
That you loved me
You loved me still the same
That you loved me
You loved me still the same

Then
    what?
            with a zip-wire trip-wire bomb-bounce big-band
Bang Bacchus fronting the Electrowercz crew
Scouts and shouts for you Ariadne it's love this
Time with a true all-over blue tattoo
And you
        <loss>
            ecstatic erratic
Torture Garden's hardened exhibits
Pour on the dance floors stimulant-silly
Bite the apple and couple and triple
And quadruple
The hand on the bottom the have you had sex yet
Brandish the fertility spike
Cover up the business end
With a pine cone, it works for some,
Juggle joints of botch-butchered bullock
Bodies bound with seething snakes
Cluster round the glass inspection
Case with the naked human inside
Thrust bold tentacles through the holes
(Tourists try to glimpse the rituals)
Spunked spanked scarlet tooth-vibrating
Tinnitus-techno here's a floorshow
The Infamous Boom Boom and Skinny Redhead
Shinbone shindig flutes with savage
Harmonics

Wait

Everything is very small
You wake up face down on the counterpane

Each tiny prick each satin stitch
Flame stitch stem stitch isolated knot
A deafening echo of embroidery thread
Dragged by a needle through a hole it made

The coverlet of panoramic rapture
Splays and displays itself around the goddess's
Chaise longue. And when the young voyeurs from Thessaly
Have gawped enough and captured all the scenes,
They surge from the immortals' roped-off paths
In human eddies, first a placid sea
Until the West Wind wrinkles it awake
And whips up towering peaks as dawn alights
On the edge of the rotating sun.
Timid, a gentle murmuring
Turns to orchestrated shouts:
Rising gusts send pulse on pulse
Coursing to lavender skies.

Once they've scattered in their homeward patterns,
First through the cordon is Chiron the Centaur, from Pelios.
He's denuded the wild of trophy flowers
The roses, red and white,
The vi'lets, and the lily-cups
Freely given by the pollinators:
Hardy field and mountain stock, the tender
Yield of river valley husbanded by
The gentle breath of gardener-god Favonius –
A jumble of artfully artless arrangements,
Their perfume makes the palace delirious.

The river god Penios checks in, fresh from the
Vale of Tempe and its lush finery,
Woods that cling to the escarpments
Given over to nymphets' silent disco.
He shows his uprooted hand of contraband
Willingly surrendered by the eco-system –
Tall slow-growing beech, fastigiate laurel,
Waving plane, sky-painting cypress, pliable black
Poplar weeping amber – tree-sister of Phaethon,
Torched when his sky-chariot obsession
Turned soil to burning dust and frozen stone.
Dying in pots, they camouflage the courtyard.

Prometheus next (whose madness for combustion
Wins approval from the biosphere),
Bearing faded scars of his old torture
Chained and dangled off a precipice.

Now the top table: father of the gods,
His dolled-up wife and more acceptable children.
Artemis and Apollo skulk at home,
Denouncing as they do the happy pair
And the ceremony's carbon footprint.

When the guests are settled in their ivory
(As before) seats, confronted by a lavish
Out-of-season banquet made of air miles,
Three little maids from school arrive, afflicted
With tremors – the Fates, here to intone the future,
Palsied bodies enfolded in white twill,
Magenta borders skimming toes,
Echoes of their incarnation
Carnation, Lily, Lily, Rose,

Rose-pink bows in silver hair, arthritic
Fingers plying labour's timeless rites:[7]

Left hand steadies the distaff with its head
Swathed in a batt of carded wool like candyfloss.
Right hand, fingers upwards, teases
Fibres into one, then thumb turned down
Twists the yarn and winds the spindle
Balanced by its base, a flattened whirling
Sphere. The tiny tufts they nibble off
To smooth the work adhere to their dry lips.
Reed baskets at their feet hold bright white
Shropshire fleeces gleaming and picked clean,
Donated by the kindness of moonlit flocks.

Sing-song prophecies they draw from thread
All come true when those unborn are dead.

NONA:
See your heroism burnished
In the setting of your virtue –
Peleus, guardian of your homeland
And the favourite of the Father,
Hear the sisters cast your fortune
On this happy day of lightness.

Threads the Fates must follow
Run with text and subtext
Through the turning tale.

---

7   In 1885 *The Mikado*, with three little maids, had its first
    performance, and John Singer Sargent began painting
    Carnation, Lily, Lily, Rose.

Spindles, twist the weft
Woven in the warp.
Time, unfold the bale.

DECIMA:
After so long without touch,
What the bridegroom craves
Is close to his embrace,
Lit by the Evening Star
Rising to meet his luck –
By your side, your wife
Waits to charm your soul
With love and share the drowsy
Peace of your dark nest,
Gentle arms a cushion
For your bull-like neck.

No home shelters such a love,
No love holds loves bound as close
As Peleus and Thetis are.

Hemp and cotton, jute and silk,
Straw, flax, grass, papyrus, reeds,
Leather, ligament, tendon, hair:
Spindles, run to twist the fibres
Into yarn that makes the strands
For cords as tight as wedding bands.

MORTA:
Born your son / void of fear
Name Achilles / enemy
See his brave / battle stare
Not his heels / never caught
Every race / outstrip deer
Burning pace

Run like fire along the fuse,
Spindles, faster than the hunted hooves

His unbeaten / hero game
Phrygia field / puddled Trojan
Soldier blood / Greek war leader
Agamemnon / clear away
Long-besieged / walls of Troy

Run with failing pulse and falling stone,
Spindles, draw the ending on

Your son honour / your son deeds
Told aloud / other mothers
Cry the cause / their own son
Funerals / hair hang down
Matted white / weak palm bruise
Emptied breast

Run with the pyre's flame, the grave's cold,
Spindles, wind thread for shrouds

Reapers scythe / tight pack rank
Stand up proud / field of gold
Fiery sun / your son cut
Swordwork harvest / Trojan men
At their peak / leave the stalk

Run with husks and severed roots,
Spindles, spin a legend with dry whispers

See his greatness / choke a river
Clog with Trojan / broken corpses
Deep Scamander / rust the colour
Clot with carnage / meet the sea
Warm with kill

Run on the river surface and the bed,
Spindles, make the bloodstained filament spread

Last exhibit / for his ghost
Let his tomb / welcome war prize
Snow white virgin / hacked to joints
After Chance / turn the tide
Dog-tired Greeks / undo Neptune
Smash the sea-wall / Troy is lost
Young bride flood / mausoleum
Your dead son / her red blood
Polyxena / Trojan princess
Crumple headless
Like a hundred sacrificial bulls.

Running from his high-placed dome,
Thread-veins, arteries, all the same

NONA:
Make it so. Be joined the way you wished.
Marriage, love, desire, souls in well-drafted
Contract, groom take goddess bride at last

And let hieromancy run
With body parts to show the unbodied time.

On the morning after, Nanny
Finds the trappings of the girl
Will not fit the newlywed.
Fretful Mummy, keen to knit
A matinée set, need not regret
A sulky daughter who won't share a bed.

Run with text and subtext,
Hem the textile island
Dyed maroon and embroidered,
Spindles, fuse the stories
In one oxblood thread.

So the Fates' involuntary
Chants foretold the joy of Peleus –

But this was in the buried age
When gods consorted with a certain class
Of human hero: bushy beards and bustles
Prowled the artists' studios of St John's
Wood and Holland Park; their standards held.
If Jupiter sauntered to his gilded
Temple to soak up the annual rites,
A hundred bulls like slaughtered brides would tumble
To the Earth – who now withholds permission
For our humble existence – but in that time
ADHD Bacchus liked to steer
His shouty dishevelled bitches from the heavens,
All Delphi surging on the road from town
To give the god a cheer and choke the air
With fumes of pasture-bred spit-roast sacrifice
While battle zones saw helmeted Mars, Athena
Or Nemesis whip the troops to wholesome killing

Until, from infra-red to ultra-violet,
The rays showed human life to be invalid.
Justice overpowered by primitive greed,
Brother's hand ran with the blood of brother,
Son saw punchlines in his parents' coffins,
Father willed his own son's early death
So that he could grab the pretty widow,
Reckless mother seduced unwitting son,
Indifferent to incest's short-lived child.

Staining good with evil in our frenzy,
We can't see the pattern or the light.
There doesn't have to be a greedy shuffling
Monster: false turns bring perpetual night.

Drag a mountain up another mountain,
Watch the death from the precarious sky,
Hear the wildfires hiss at welling oceans –
This, the work we'll be forgotten by.

No more plough rust
No more skin dust
No more cherry-coloured
Twist

Playlist
I hear the soft note of the echoing voice from *Patience*, W.S. Gilbert and Arthur Sullivan; *I dreamt I dwelt in marble halls* from *The Bohemian Girl*, Michael William Balfe and Alfred Bunn; *Ace of Spades*, Motörhead

65

The invitation's better than the waltz.
Wheeling over water beats the splashdown.
The seducer's happier in bed
With a good book.
Muses ghost me.

Although I'm too worn down by loss to tangle with
Those clever girls who feed me their ideas,
Hórtalus, and my best work is aborted
While I watch sadness spreading like a bruise –

The flood tide of oblivion lapped
At my defenceless brother's bloodless foot.
Bundled underground, unregarded,
He lies smothered on the coast of Troy

<*loss*>

Then nothing? Brother, my death was yours to play with,
But what was loved must always call for love
And I will always chant my grief to you
As the mythic mother turned to nightingale
Sings from darkened leaves for the son she killed –

Still, Hortalus, I'm sending you the lees
Of mourning: my attempt at Callimachus,
In case you feared your request was tossed to
Random winds by my preoccupation

Like the secret gift, a round sweet apple
Sent by boy to girlfriend, stowed away –
Look, I'm back to my old self,
Slipping inside a careless virgin's dress –
Mother walks in, girl jumps up, it tumbles
Out, her cheeks flush guilty, it bounces
Across the floor, the bruises spread like sadness.

The girl alone in her bedroom with Radio Caroline
On her transistor radio, whose mother
Would never knock, snatched up something too late
And stuffed it down her jumper.
In the tirade that followed over the music
She thought her mother accused her of eating Cox's.

66 [8]

Clickety click

For Joy, Teddie and Babs, the Beverley Sisters

And with his bloody great radio telescope
He picked up every heavenly body
On Saturday nights at the Atalanta Ballroom
In Woking,[9] the centre of the known world
At that time.

He plotted stars as they were born and faded,
Solar eclipses on the Ambre Solaire,
The passing of the Lockheed Constellations[10]
Turn! Turn! Turn![11] *Wild thing, I think you move me*[12]
And forecast when Diana, the Moon herself,
Would cycle out of time for a tryst behind
The Princess of Wales near the Six Crossroads Roundabout.[13]

He being Conon, the Astronomer Royal

And he found me

---

8   Catullus's translation from Greek of what is now a fragmentary
    part of the *Aetia* by the erudite, allusive poet Callimachus
    (third century BC).
9   Town in south-east England
10 Airliners
11 By Pete Seeger, popularised by the Byrds, 1965
12 From *Wild Thing* by Chip Taylor, popularised by the Troggs, 1966
13 Road junction outside Woking

Eight Miles High[14] pointed at *Telstar*[15]
Years before *Stairway to Heaven*.[16]

I being a lock of hair bleached platinum
Snipped from Queen Berenice's[17] lacquered beehive –

She with her outstretched arms sugared smooth at the salon
Dedicating me to Dusty Springfield,
Diana Dors, Johnny Hallyday[18]
And Mandy Rice-Davies[19] defended by Bobby Moore.[20]

This queen's new hedge-fund, pardon me, husband, King
   Ptolemy
Had just set off to point some nukes at the enemy,
Proud of his bruises from their wedding night
(I think 'despoiling a virgin' is wide of the mark).

Oh, and those battling old-time brides
Just after the reception –
Did they really fend off sex?
Or was it to spite their parents' hopes
With lakes of fake tears in the matrimonial suite?

I swear that's all just amateur dramatics.
Her Majesty taught me this with her convincing
Sobs when her new hatstand went off to make war.

---

14   The Byrds, 1966
15   By Joe Meek for the Tornados, 1962
16   Led Zeppelin, 1971
17   Berenice II, wife of her cousin Ptolemy III, King of Egypt
18   Singer, actress, singer, blonde/blond
19   Blonde in the Profumo affair
20   Blond captain (centre-back) of the England football team who
     won the 1966 FIFA World Cup

Whether your wailing was for the empty bed, Ma'am,
Or more like sisterly feeling, you nearly collapsed –
Right into *They're Coming To Take Me Away, Ha-haaa!*,[21]
19th Nervous Breakdown[22] territory –

Still, ever since you were small, you've been, er, resourceful.
Remember your wholly justifiable scheme
To hook yourself a royal wedding? Only
Someone as hard as shellac would have risked it.
Here's the write-up in *Jennifer's Diary*:[23] you murdered
Your has-been-to-be, your first one, to make yourself Queen
Of Egypt. But he was your mother's lover
Which made it OK
I suppose.

Your farewell to your current Hansard was…touching.
Then you wept through a box of Kleenex, stacking
Stupid Cupid[24] and *Baby Come Back*[25] on the turntable.
You got pissed on Bull's Blood and – back to the temple –
Promised me to Twinkle, Kathy Kirby,
Jackie Trent, Joan Sims and Barbara Windsor[26]
If only they'd let your adored house band survive

---

21 Napoleon XIV (Jerry Samuels), 1966
22 The Rolling Stones, 1966
23 Glossy magazine society column
24 Connie Francis, 1958
25 The Equals, 1966
26 Respectively singer-songwriter, singer, singer-songwriter,
    actress, actress, all blonde

And bingo,
He turns up out of the Shadows and the Tornados,[27]
Filling the deities' book of Green Shield stamps[28]
So they could claim me as a gift.

I didn't like being hacked from your updo, Ma'am.
Hated it, I swear by your Carmen rollers.
Anyone making such a statement lightly
Should get the comb-out they deserve

But who's a match for carbon steel blades?
If they can make soft landings on the Moon
How can hair resist industrial forces
Even with Elnett Satin?
Damn the boring ore-mongers, damn blast furnaces.

While the left-behind locks mourned my departure
I lay on the altar of goddess-queen Arsinoë
Who'd had the Aphrodite makeover
After her death when she finally changed her stylist.
She set the West Wind's diffuser dryer to cool,
Wafted me to Venus's wholesome lap

Then – to give Ariadne's bridal tiara,
Corona Borealis, competition
In heaven's walk of fame, and to display
My full-beam Goldilocks dazzle,
Damp as I was from sea-spray on the journey
Now I'd reached Vidal Sassoon[29] at last –
Venus took me past Hitchcock *Blonde on Blonde*[30]

---

27 Beat groups
28 Shopping loyalty scheme
29 Eponymous trend-setting hair salon
30 Bob Dylan, 1966

Doris Day, Grace Kelly and Janet Leigh[31]
To set me down, the newest star.

31   Three stars of Alfred Hitchcock films

You can call me Coma Berenices.
I'm right by the Fanny Cradock[32] illuminations,
Lenny the Lion and Sooty,[33]
Running ahead of the dozy cowman Boötes
Who sinks under candlewick bedspread and eiderdown,

But though I dance with gods in Annabel's[34]
All night, returning to Tethys the sea goddess
At dawn (that grey bob suits her, by the way),
I hope you'll let me speak out, Lady Nemesis,
Even if my horoscope says it's dangerous –

I'm not exactly thrilled by any of this.
Cropped and chopped forever from Mistress's head –
It's torture.

Conditioner, madam? Sorry, it's a reflex,
But while we're on the subject, before her engagement
Mistress didn't buy high-end hair hydrators
So I was forced to choke down cheap generics and –

Oh no, it's the cheeky sales rep. He always butts in.

Ladies! On your long-awaited honeymoon
Don't give in to your Brylcreemed other half
In your see-thru Bri-Nylon® babydoll
Until you've applied these silky luxury brands
Which look so smart on your onyx vanity unit.

As for those who run around having affairs –

---

32 TV cook
33 TV puppets, the latter a bear
34 Mayfair club

I hope your curls frizz up in a tragic home perm
But I'll take your number.
Now, happy brides should reach for this Harmony range –

And you too, Ma'am:
When you lie back and think of the Zodiac
Doing your wifely duty with the lights on,
Don't leave me crisp and shrivelled under a hairnet:
Make the other stars envy your royal barnet
Or vanish into black holes on *The Sky at Night.* [35]

If I could only return to the Queen's Head in Byfleet, [36]
Let the Age of Aquarius do what it likes.
Next year comes the Summer of Love, and Hair.[37]

---

35   Long-running British TV programme
36   Pub near Woking
37   Love-rock musical, 1967 (Gerome Ragni, James Rado, Galt
     MacDermot)
     When the moon is in the Seventh House
     And Jupiter aligns with Mars
     Then peace will guide the planets
     And love will steer the stars.
     This is the dawning of the age of Aquarius...

67

What's in and out and banging?
A door!

Yeah this is like the one about the bridge,
The old up and over.
No, I wouldn't say I trivialise things,
Quite the opposite

So here's the dream – with lots of my specials:
Betrayal, genitalia, towers, vegetables,
My home town, urination, virgins, money.
All that's missing is the mule.

No, not her, I mean an actual mule.

Now, what's more reassuring to a
Nice bland hubby and his bride's parents than –
Oh hello, stout front Door with a good thick bolt.
May the freeholder grant you a nice lick of varnish.
I hear you kept it shut for old man Balbus
When he lived here, but you came unhinged
Once he was a goner and his heir
Moved in with the new wife.

Then Door lets in a draught of words,
An entrance entranced with itself:

'Not guilty, with due respect to the owner Caecilius –
But when there's bother
The riff-raff call out, "Door, it's all your fault."'

Your word against theirs. Can you make it stand up?

'How? No one cares.'

(Door needs oiling.) Oh yes we do.

'Well, that stuff about her being carried
Over my threshold a virgin is balls.
Her first husband didn't touch her
With that appendage which never reached an acute
Angle (wilted chard was harder),
But to ruin the unhappy home
His dad scored a hole in one –
Either he couldn't control his disgusting urges
Or the son was gelded
And someone had to whip out a length of gristle
To get her clothes off and continue the line.'

Yeah you're wearing your romance-is-dead look
But that's what I put in my dream diary word for word
So I'll carry on if you don't mind. I say to Door:
What a great example of paternal devotion
To piss through his son's keyhole.

Door runs with the theme:
'The gentle golden stream flows by the banks of
Brescia under the watchtower – a desirable
Location which gave rise to my own dear Verona –
And it was on Brescia CCTV
That she opened her letterbox to Postumius.
And Cornelius.

Some may ask, in between knob jokes,
How I'm wise to the action, being a fixture?

Well, I vibrate to her furtive whispers
With the domestics – she thinks I'm a block of wood.
And there's another notch on her bedpost
But if I name him he'll give me a hammering.
Ginger. Tall. Got sued in a
High-rolling false paternity case.'

Yeah I know that shitshow,
The Phantom of the Pregnancy.
And I've worked out who he is.
Go on, guess.
Oh sorry, I didn't notice the time.
I'll think of a good knock-knock gag for next week.

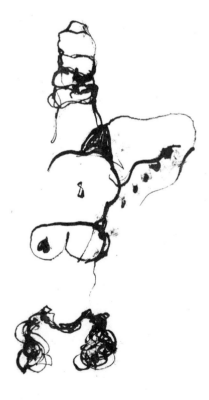

68

Floorwork

You write to me tearful castaway gasping
foam seethes drowned wreck cling neck
demand my kiss of life
goddess of sex has you wakeful
marooned on narrow mattress raging
inflamed can't be calmed by classic writers
the old reliable thumb-sucking lullabies –
I'm touched it's me you turn to
For words of consolation and love
But I'm stranded too –
No blessing left in my pockets

The minute I was legal
I dazzled, grabbed it all,
Flowers, nettles,
Pain and the pleasure of pain. The frenzy stopped
Dead with my brother's death.
Oh my brother I couldn't keep you safe
I wear black in your endless wake
Your grave our house now
The joy I rooted in your love rotten

My mind can't break for the surface.
You say I piss away time here in Verona
While the alpha male clambers on top of her
In the bed I deserted –
You misread me. Grief holds me down,
Stultifies a gift of words. No flow of writers here.

I left them in Rome; now just half a shelf.
Don't think I'm sulking or lying,
Keeping back books or love.
I'm icebound
Or I would come.

68 (B)

Eight transitions

Muses, unpeg my tongue.
Time mustn't scribble over
What Allius did for me.
I'll hold him above the dark tide
something missing/go on
The spider at work in the cornice
Won't blur his inscription with cobwebs.

You saw the hate-love torture
Cauterise me like lava
Or boiling springs,
My cheeks striated with tears,
But just as water tumbles
To relieve the parched valley
And soft breath answers storm-vexed
Prayers in the dark pumping vortex,
That's how Allius helped me –
Spreading a gangway of flowers on broad dry land
He gave us a safe house for sex
Where I waited for Mistress's
Shimmering goddess aura,
The click of heels on worn tiles.
Her threshold pause

And matching her, love-fixated
Long-dead Laodamia skirted the scaffolding
To enter the house of her bridegroom Protesilaus
(First to spring to the fight and be cut down) –
The unblessed shell unfinished like the marriage
Badly begun without blood sacrifice
(Always make me check the rubric
Before I commit) – but Laodamia learned
The altar's fascination with gore
Before she had time for enough or too much sex
With the one-day husband dragged from her arms
When the Helen grab set Greece on Troy

The deadly Middle East sump, Troy
Humanity's acrid ash, Troy
The stop to my brother's life.
These tears are for my brother taken mid-flight,
My brother, the family's best hope
Rammed in its tomb.
We died with you. Our happiness
Fed on your love's honey.
You are down with anonymous dead
In Troy's distant filth

Where the pick of the Greeks
Deserting their firesides
Pricked Paris's dream
Of wallowing with the adulteress
And widowhood took you
At beauty's peak, Laodamia.
You'd plunged to love's core –
Here's Arcadia's flood pit
Dug by Hercules mining
The soft parts beneath the mons

When man-eating birds were his bull's-eyes
And he was a king's slave
Parting heaven's gates
To marry the goddess of being young

But your love bored deeper than this.
Tamed by dominance
You loved him more than the rich man loves his grandchild
Born in time to disinherit the distant
Relative poised like a comedy vulture –
More than the frantic snowy dove
Adores the mate she pecks in a kissing frenzy –
Your headlong passion outstripped theirs
As you clung to your blond hero

And with desire as fierce as yours – possibly –
Mistress came to me burnished
With Cupid's saffron glow.
She isn't satisfied with just the one Catullus of course
Among her (few) conspirators.
In her position one doesn't bestow
Exclusivity
But it would be otiose to object –
Watch me, I'm Juno, queen of heaven,
Holding the lid on her boiling rage
While Jupiter puts it about…
Not that it's OK to compare gods with mortals
the connection was lost here/no it wasn't
Don't harp on like a doddery parent – it's thankless.
And she wasn't exactly given away to me
By a doting father in front of
Scented lilies in serried arrangements,
But on a night of miracles
She smuggled in what scraps she could offer stolen

From an actual husband's actual bed.
It's enough if she weighs her hours with me like diamonds

So, Allius, for services rendered
Take a home-made poem to rust-proof your name.
Be happy, you and your woman,
The house where we could play at being married
this bit's rusty/drop it
And far above everyone else
The woman who casts the light.
I love her more than life, I live
Through her, touch happiness through her.

69

Rufus asks:

Dear Pythia

Why won't women let me lie on top of them
Even for a Net-a-Porter account
Or a very slightly included Bulgari diamond?

PYTHIA SAYS:
Everyone knows you're disgusting.
That toxic goat
Armpit stink
Chokes the pretty ones
And the ugly ones

Poor people use baking soda and lemon juice
But you can afford Botox
To block the sweat

And if you won't do that
Don't even think about soixante-neuf
Creep

70

She says she wouldn't marry
Anyone but me
Even if God Almighty
Got down on one knee.

Her words. But what a woman
Tells a rampant lover
Scrolls out on the wind
And the swollen river.

71

Isn't it miraculous –
If anyone deserved a curse
Doubled, gout and armpit goat,
It's him, your rival for her strolling attentions.

When he gets to fuck her
She has to die or hold her nose
While uric acid sears his toes.

You dwell on that to avoid
The question of her choosing him.

72

When I saw everything through gauze
You said 'I'm yours' and made me king.
I prized you – not just as a male
Grabs his polyester bride
But as a lion loves his pride.

Now I see with unstreaked eyes,
Your squalid lies turn up the flame.
You ask 'How come?' *As if you didn't* –
Because the talons in the wound
Make the lover more feverish, less kind.

73

They won't break your fall but they smash up everything else.
They let your harness slip so you hang by your neck –
All of them, all of the time.

Your generous acts get spat right back.
They cut you down to smack the floor with your face.

Take my case.
The one who got the gold for cruelty
And put my life in a choke-hold
Had said, 'No one but you. My only friend.'

74

You know Gellius's uncle?
Gets off on giving people verbal spankings
For saucy output.

Gellius says no thanks, pulls uncle's wifey,
Turns him Trappist overnight.

Now Gellius can shove his dick down that man's throat
As much as he likes and probably does –
Uncle won't get a word out.

No I haven't got better things to do
But I'm glad you have.

75

This is what we've come to, Clodia. My
Self-will has been dragged down by the beast in you and
Drowned in its own pool of meaning well.

I couldn't bring myself to like you now
Even if you played the convent girl

Or give up loving you, no matter how
Wide you spread your legs to the whole world.

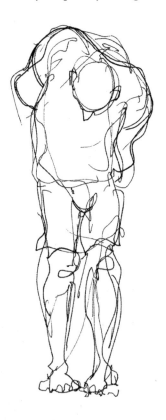

76

Intra-Venus

What does being honest feel like?
If you keep a faithful note
Of how you avoid the crooked route,
There's comfort when your hair's gone white
[Don't bother, you won't make it – Ed.]
Salvaged from this obsessive blight.

What altruism says or does,
You've said, done, and been called
A prick for it. Accept the pain.
The vein's collapsed. Rip out the line.

It's hard to abandon a love that runs a life

But hanging on will hurt you more.
Here are twelve steps and a door.

If anyone knows what pity is, if you've waltzed
Someone away from the edge,
Watch me – and if you see gold in my sad river,
Save me from being a burning, boring addict.

My love is not reflected in her eyes.
Ask her where she's been and she tells lies.
I want to be released from this
Corrosive habit.
I had integrity. Please.

77

Well, Captain Scarlet.
That went nowhere, our zero-sum game.
It was looking like friendship from here.

Did I say nowhere? Here's my heart crashing
Into the red, hijacked by grief.

Was this your plan – play the blood-brother,
Barbecue my certainties to a *saignant* crimson,

Do your superhero swoop
To grab it all out of my arms?

You stole my life.

I weep for how you seeded my arteries,
Weep for our closeness that came with a fatal condition.

78

Here's a shock, my old cock. Your brother's wife
Knocking your other brother's son.

Her nephew-in-law. Look, I'll draw you a diagram.

They're sexed-up grown-ups and it isn't incest for once
But get you, lining the schlocky love-nest,
Probably by mistake – what a blockhead
Helping a jock pick the wedlock
Bedrock lock stock and ad hoc to mock an uncle
And you married.

78 (B)

<*loss*>

But now I can't give it a rest. Imagining it.
Her virtuous virginal kisses
Slimed with your pissy snail trail.
You'll never be free.
I'll scrawl it on the longest-lasting walls
Whatever your name is.

79

Brother/switch
Sister/bitch
Pretty Clodius is the catch
So Clodia will hitch him close,
Cut loose the poet and his rope family –

But let Sir Pretty of the Clan McPretty
Give those rope orphans to unattractive Masters
If he can beg three single-column ties
Eins zwei drei
From those who know what he plies

The family name of Clodia and her brother Clodius was Pulcher (handsome).

80

When icicles hang by the wall
And Dick the shepherd blows

Snowflakes that stay
On my nose and eyelashes
I can't concentrate at all

Serissa foetida Mount Fuji
The snow rose

To frost a margarita glass:
Minced jalapeños, lime zest and coarse salt

With patients who won't crawl past oral
Boredom cuts my powdery notes

Patient C has obsessive thoughts about Gellius.
Describes him:
Rose-hip lips whiter than toothpaste
When he's spotted first thing
And then emerges dull from whiling away
A distended afternoon.
(What does C do all day?)

C's fantasy:
High peaking volcano man
Erupts on Gellius's soft palate
Man called Victor
Or maybe is a victor
But a cheap one

I'm Frankenstein on the coruscating glacier
Monster incoming
He bounded over the crevices in the ice
I'd like to point out that it should be crevasses
But if I mention asses he'll take off
His only use of the c-word regards a mule

Gellius's rimed rimmed lips –
Wet nurse envy?
Ask C if his mother wore pearl necklaces

C stops talking at last to eat
A pack of fun-size Milky Way

8₁

Couldn't you find a decent rigger, Juventius,
Instead of the spray-tanned poser from Watford
Who's binding you now? How dare you prefer
His ropes to mine?
You don't know
How stupid you look, dangling and spinning like that.

Catullus takes a metropolitan swipe at Pisaurum, now Pesaro and
twinned with Watford.

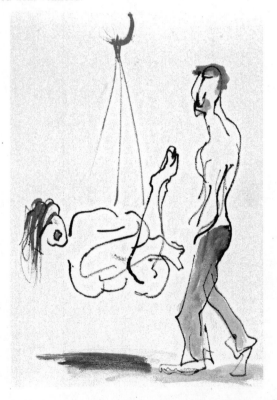

82

Look at me, Quintius.
If you want me to believe
I'd sacrifice my eyesight for your sake,
Or something even more precious than these eyes,

Don't force us apart.

Believe I love her more than I love these eyes,
More than I love the gifts more precious than sight.

83

Clodia lingers over all my faults
For hubby's benefit. He laps it up.

Twat. Cat got your brain?

If she could blot out what we share
Shut that mouth
She'd be over it

But her epic monologue
Is a mnemonic
For me

And worse than that to goad her on

The needle in the skin
Concentrated acid on the tongue

84

'a pleasantly trivial anecdote ridiculing the pretensions of an upstart'

The Oxford Anthology of Roman Literature

Haspirations, says 'Arry.
He's got plenty of those,

All that gusty huffing –
Fighting with bows and harrows
Makes his ardour harder.

Gets it from his mother
And jumped-up hancestors
With hairs instead of heirs.

How our ears rejoiced
At his posting overseas
Then closed up with distaste
When we heard about Haitch R Haitch –

Wipe that look off your face.
This pleasant enough for you?
Were you at the other place?

85

Odi et amo. quare id faciam, fortasse requiris?
nescio, sed fieri sentio et excrucior.

Hate I/hating I and love I/loving I. By what thing it do I/doing
I perhaps enquire you/enquiring you

Not know I/not knowing I but to happen/to be happening feel I/
feeling I and tortured I/tortured I am being

I hate where I do love. Perchance
Thou seek'st to know *de quelle façon*
[Doffs hat, strums lute-strings].
I don't know. It's hurting. *Here.*

Hate-love-hate-love you ask why the needle's stuck
I can't say but the pain is an endless track

HATE/WANT. Since you've got to ask –
Me neither. But [because?] it's torture.

I'm in love with loathing. You demand reasons
I can't give. But they're real, the hooks in my flesh.

Attraction-repulsion. You shove your probe right in.
[shrug] It's a vocation, having my liver plucked out.

Stuck in a hate-love trap.
'How does it make you feel?'
Don't give me that counselling crap.
Wheels have spikes. Bones snap.

86

And *that's* supposed to be beautiful –
Pulling the milkshake limbs out straight and long.
Boring.
You get points for technique
But they don't add up to beauty.

Your bland suspension
Has no magic,
No pinch of suffering passivity,
No hurt, no sweat.

Now look at mine.
There's blinding beauty in that tie,
More than yours or anybody's,
Executed with tricks I took from the best.

87

No woman can attest that she
Is in receipt of love to the degree
Assigned to Lesbia by me

No contract holds as tightly as the force of
Love that binds me to your claws

88, 89, 90

Pub bore

What do you make of that, Gellius?
A man who does his mother and his sister?
Rolling around all night with no clothes on.
And his aunt.
Off the scale, would you say, Gellius?
There's only so much whitewash
And that image
I can't exorcise,
A self-fellating coil.
See you
Around yourself.

Go ahead, the seat's free.
You might not recognise Gellius over there
After the massive weight loss.
His mother's so accommodating
And fit for her age,
His sister's hot,
His uncle cooperates and
There's a troupe of girl cousins –
No wonder he's skin and bone.
Even confining himself to 'display only' goods
And nothing legit
Keeps him all ribs.

I thought I'd ordered medium rare. Doesn't this
Make you think of Gellius and his mother?
Oh really? Well listen,
They've got a baby on the way.
All their illegal shagging
In that filthy cult –
They'll spawn an actual magus,
Aleister Crowley kind of thing.
Junior will be a souped-up thurifer
Jabbering the mumbo jumbo,
Flinging fatty offal on the pyre –

What am I saying,
He won't reach term.
They'll barbecue the foetus bits
And call it faggots in caul.

91

No, Gellius.
That's not why I hoped you'd stay onside
In my pitiful, pitiless affair.
It wasn't my X-ray eyes, or trust, or believing
That you could keep your mind off sex for a second –

No. It was because she wasn't your mother.
Or your sister.

My love for her gnawed like cancer.

I thought the fact that you and I were friends
Wouldn't be enough to unbind your hands.
And look what happened. You love to boost your frail
Member in the compost of betrayal.

92

Clodia slanders me on oath
Can't be forced to shut her mouth
So Clodia loves me *by Almighty*
God. What is the proof? I'm just the
Same – I'd string her up but I'm
In love with her *whole truth and nothing*

93

And your mother

I can't be arsed to please you, Caesar.
Your hide could be white or black for all I care.

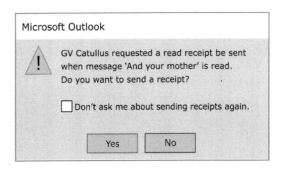

At the time of writing, the Microsoft Outlook read-receipt pop-up gives dominance to the recipient, who can read without acknowledging receipt.

94

Mister Man-Tool's an adulterer.

An adulterer?

Yeah, is there an echo in here?
You know what Lewis and Short[38] says:
'The pot culls its own herbs.'

Who? What? You mean pot kettle black?

No.

Skunk?

---

38   Latin dictionary; see definition of *olla*.

95, 95 (B)

FIRST CITIZEN: *Tear him to pieces; he's a conspirator.*
CINNA: *I am Cinna the poet, I am Cinna the poet.*
FOURTH CITIZEN: *Tear him for his bad verses, tear him for his
bad verses.*
CINNA: *I am not Cinna the conspirator.*

Shakespeare, *Julius Caesar*

Sylvia, now in hardback
By my own dear Cinna,
Nine years in the making,
Out in time for Christmas –

Meanwhile
<it's breaking up>
With half a million *<sold? words? units of currency?>*
In one *<offshore account? e-book? week?>*
Hortensius
<try a different channel>

Sylvia, instant classic, film rights auctioned –
Sylvia, analysed for centuries
While Mr Voluble's remaindered
Annals are shipped quietly abroad,
Just so much chip paper.

Five stars for my friend's
Small volume of lasting importance –
You won't pluck Cinna's name out of my heart –

And one star for the flatulent Antimachus
Who sells in millions.

Never heard of him? You've made my day.

PS it didn't work out that way.
Cinna, lucky bastard, got a death scene
In that play, the one about You-Know-Who.
Sylvia was left behind, apart from

Your tears at daybreak were lit by raking dawn;
A little time to wait and your tears at dusk
Glittered at the touch of the evening star...

But what she'd tricked her daddy into planting
Started to weigh down Sylvia's uterus

96

If the silent coffin space
Can find sustenance
In our grief, Calvus, which shares a seam
Of longing with loves we once
Knew and need to feel again
And with tears we cry
For deep commitment cast away,
Quintilia does not grieve
Her death that was too soon but lies
Enraptured by your love.

97

Dear Membership Secretary

Why the hell did you let Aemilius join?
His breath smells of arse.
Both ends lack personal care
But I'd back the arse – it's got no fangs
And it's sweeter than his snaggled NHS tombstones,
Periodontal disease laid out on a rusty
Nissan chassis –

Right, he's off:
Open wide, it's like the slack cunt of a
Mule pissing into the Sirocco –
Fucks his bitches – pick-up artist
Dodging a community service order
Back at the donkey sanctuary
Blah blah, C's recurring fantasy,
That belle de jour he brings in here
Rimming a syphilitic slaughterman –

Sadly his direct debit turns up like clockwork.
We'll never get rid of him that way.

98

Dear Membership Secretary,

I can't believe
Victius asked me to sponsor his application.

He's a smelly windbag and a gusset-sniffing arse-licker
Guzzling off the caked soles of pound-shop shit-kickers.

When his mouth is open
The toxins
Empty the bar
In seconds.
Cheers.

99

I couldn't stop myself
You were helpless in my ropes
The smell of you
Juventius listen
It was the best

But I didn't get away with it.
You hauled me up and strung me out
Inverted crucifix
For more than sixty minutes.
I sobbed and said sorry
But you left me transfixed.

I'd barely untied you
Before you ran to wash yourself
And flicked away the water with your delicate hands
Scared I'd infect you
With crack-whore juice.

You sacrificed me to your fury
Spatchcocked
And reconditioned my reflex
To make that moment more explosive than
The world's worst emetic.

If this is your revenge on a hard Master
I'll never help myself again.

Verona's hottest boys
Scouting for new owners
Score a sibling act.
Caelius picks the brother,
Quintius the other –
Cute fraternal pact.

Which one gets the kudos?
Caelius, it's you –
Bonded as we are,
Hardened in the fire
When that Mistress phase
Torched my sanity.
Caelius, stay lucky,
Beat the casino at love.

101

Flight-shamed through the earthbound ports and checkpoints
I'm here, brother, for this bleak ceremony,
To help you fathom death's assembly kit
And offer useless words to wordless ashes.
I wasn't strong enough to keep hold of you.
Now I'll never find the missing piece

Here are the conventional sad tokens
For the old rituals that told us so.
Take them sea-splashed with a brother's tears
And for ever like the tide, my brother,
I come to claim you and to let you go

102

If you want a human safe deposit
For the closest secrets of your heart
Gagging to be served a gagging order –
You're looking at him.

I'll print a tidy quatrain just to hint at it
In foreign editions down millennia.
You won't begrudge this hedge against obscurity
When I can't monetise posterity.

No one will know who you are or what I'm on about.
Cross my heart, Cornelius,
And hope to die.

Hide your conscience in an uncracked eggshell,
Let me keep it safe, Cornelius,
You can trust me not to make a pinhole.

103

Be so gracious as to
Give back that 10k
I paid for shoddy leaky
Girlfriends for the night,
Silo, and enjoy
Your vicious thug life –

Or if you'd rather shag the
Cash then be my guest but
Don't be a vicious thug
Pimp.

104

You think I cursed the woman
More central to me than my brain stem?

If I could reach so low
I wouldn't be lost in trackless love for her.

You bastards want to pull down all the cathedrals.

105

Mister Man-Tool struggled with digital currencies. Hodlers ignored his tips. His wallets got hacked.

106

When you see an auctioneer
With a boy from the reception desk
Don't you think he yearns to be a
Hot lot number entered in the catalogue
Under a really big hammer?

107

Breaking

If the single object of hope and longing
Can be possessed with the snap of a wishbone it's…

Welcome.
Welcome back. You're what I've longed for,
More than the big cash prize, and you've *come back,*
Clodia, come back to me on a bone's crack,

I've longed for

Back

Oh this is a day of delirium.
Who's happier than I am? Who can think
That I'll have any further need for hope?

Dear Pythia

Will my fantasies come true?

I don't like Cominius
He's a disgusting pensioner
Probably a nonce
So I want to
Razor slivers off his tongue
Flick them at a starving vulture
Set a carrion crow to peck his
Eyeballs out and glug them down
Chuck his guts to dogs
Feed his leftover bits
Out of plastic bags
To wolves in the zoo
It's the will of the people

And I want to meet Lydia
Because she wrote
the wolves they are so smart
we was throwing big stick to them
and they where playing
but u arnt allowed to do tht
so dont get caught lol

PYTHIA SAYS:
Ring Narcotics Anonymous
And try cognitive
Behavioural therapy, arsehole

109

Lockdown

Our special place.
Yes Mistress.
You're dangling
Our love affair
As a fixture, you and me, I can nearly –

Please Mistress

No mistrust. Make her mean it
Straight from the heart with no slick coating
So that we can formalise the thing
In a mystic tantric bond of transcendental –

Yes Mistress

Aufillena, good girls get credit.
They check the small print, take a big hint,
Open wide, get astride,
Finish what they started.

You tell lies and break our contract,
Grab the advance and never follow through.

Put out or copy nice girls, Aufillena.
They don't promise candid interviews.

Raking in the cash on false pretences
Is criminal greed. Give me a straight-up whore
Who lays it all out on the tray with no taboo.

Search term: Pornhub

111

Aufillena, a bride who keeps
Her vows is like the Holy Mother

But better shag a queue of creeps
Than breed your cousins with Daddy's brother.

112

Mister Septum, few men head
For your salad buffet spread

Although you're versatile
And take it up the aisle

113

When I started out, Cinna,
Maecilia had two men on the go.

Now I'm twice as old she's grafted
Hundreds on each one and watched them grow.

Adultery, rampant in the polytunnel.

114, 115

Mister Man-Tool's big in Firmum –
What a country estate.
Fish, feather, pasture,
Arable and hunting –

Burns up all the profit
But I'll call him rich
With that balance sheet
Primed for tax avoidance.

Waggles his length of pasture,
Strip for ploughing,
Saltmarsh lick –

Can't believe he's not worth more
Than Croesus gold in every pore,
All those massive holdings in one hand –

Grazing, cropping, stretched-out woods,
Vacant bogs from north to south,
What a big allotment plot
But he overshadows it,
Looming, monstrous Mister Man-Tool.

No I can do this

Wait

116

So much and for your sake
I brought my mind to bear
On how to render the Greek
Old master[39] for your ear.

I read him raw
And sang his sweet remains outside your door
To soften you towards me and to charm
Away your naked thought of doing me harm.

Now I see my time
Wasted on this task,
Gellius, my prayer
Crumpled on the floor.

Your pale critique is helpless in my wake.
Pinioned by me you will receive, not take.

---

39   Callimachus

116 (B) [40]

I was all the birds of Callimachus:

The crane at the jugular,[41]
The unknown predator,[42]
The vagrant shearwater,[43]
The flick knife kingfisher,[44]

The birds of omen,[45]
Every forsaken
Immortal nightingale,[46]
The stork with revenge in mind,[47]
The crow on the roof that croaks,
'What the hell happens next?'[48],
The eagle with a word
From Zeus,[49] Apollo's swan
Winging it,[50]

---

40 There is no 116 (B).
41 Callimachus, *Aetia* Book I line 14 (all numbering from Loeb, 2022)
42 Aetia Book II 43ª 43.61
43 Epigram 58
44 Epigram 5 line 10
45 Hymn V lines 123-4
46 Epigram 2
47 *Hecale* 76
48 Fragments of Epigrams 1b
49 Hymn I line 68
50 Hymn II line 5

The monumental bronze cock[51]

And after me
Look out for your three ravens sat on a tree,[52]
A darkling thrush under the canopy.[53]

Don't keep your sparrow waiting in the mead-hall.[54]

Maybe you'll find it all.[55]

51   Epigram 56
52   *The Three Ravens*, English traditional ballad
53   *The Darkling Thrush*, Thomas Hardy, chosen to open
     The Harvill Book of Twentieth-Century Poetry in English
     (Harvill, 1999) by its editor Michael Schmidt
54   Image from Bede, *Ecclesiastical History of the English People*,
     Book II, Chapter XIII
55   See you later annotator.

THE LAGER CATULLUS [56]

Stella six-pack
And Hellas Verona
Yeah Greek boys
Can't avoid 'em
Beating the crap out of Roma on Sky
That'll be the day
Kiss my arse
Kiss me
You're the boss
I love it
I hate it
Hate wanting
Want hating
Hate myself
Hate you more
I love my brother
Come back
[Crying]
It's the parents' expectations
You owe me money
You're shit poets
You shag anything
She won't put out
Even though I paid her
And that pimp
Hand down my joggers
You're disgusting

---

56   I misread the working title for this book, *The Larger Catullus*.
     Catullus's local football team, Hellas Verona ('Greece Verona'),
     won a championship in 1985 but is surpassed by Roma.

He cut his off
All by himself
You've got to laugh
We're a movement
Are we?
You cheated me
OK I was lying
Keep your filthy dick out of my boyfriend
I owe you nothing
You can't read
I didn't mean I'd *really* do that
You stole my gear
They can't get possession
It's incest
Well you try galliambics then
Give me all the feelings
Beauty is truth truth something
No I prefer Marlboros
Can't move for wedding invitations
Wish I'd got Corona in
Wish I'd got in
Yeah a nice boat
Then it's over in a few seconds
Kissing goes on longer
Sail away
I got shafted at work
But I don't need the pension
Don't need not won't need
Why won't you love me?
That's a horrible pass
You ripped off the whole country
Her husband has no idea
She's a slag anyway
Have you read this by Callimachus

Look it's really good
What's the point
Wasting my time
Time
Oh no
Penalties

I find a two-term weekly class on Catullus textual criticism. I email Stephen Harrison, Professor of Latin Literature at Oxford. May I attend as a graduate of this establishment? 'It's rather austere,' he warns. But I would like to peer at the living conjecture about what Catullus wrote.

His works survive through one incomplete manuscript, shot with mistakes (not his), which bobbed up in about 1300, was copied, and vanished again. Since the Renaissance a stream of scholars, including A.E. Housman, have been on the unachievable quest for authenticity.

One fourteenth-century scribe was so concerned about the wretched state of the material that he wrote a note (in the third person) asking for the reader's pardon: '… in order to assemble something from this rough and ready source, he decided that it was better to have it in a corrupt state than not to have it at all, while hoping still to be able to correct it from another copy which might happen to emerge. Fare you well, if you do not curse him.'

That translation from the Renaissance Latin is by Professor Harrison.[57] Subtly hand-jiving fragments of the poems, he runs the class jointly with Professor Stephen Heyworth.

Today Dr Tristan Franklinos canters through the variants in poem 69. For example, the third line begins with a meaningless *nos illa mare* (we or us/her or that/sea) found in the three oldest surviving manuscripts. They are in the Bodleian Library in Oxford, the Bibliothèque nationale de France and the Biblioteca Apostolica Vaticana.

Contenders include the widely accepted Renaissance version *non si illam* **rarae** (not if...her...fine...), *non si illam* **carae** (expensive), and *non si illam* **Coae** (of a female prostitute or of the Coan moth – that is, fine silk). With the rest of the line it could mean: 'Even if you try to seduce her with pricey labels...'

Like a successful virus, a single corrupted anthology, emanating by chance, continues to be replicated and is improved in the process. As centuries pass it becomes more or less widespread according to the cultural climate.

Time longer than rope
    Jamaican proverb

---

57 'The Need for a New Text of Catullus' in *Vom Text zum Buch*, ed. C. Reitz (Sankt Katharinen, 2000), 63–79.

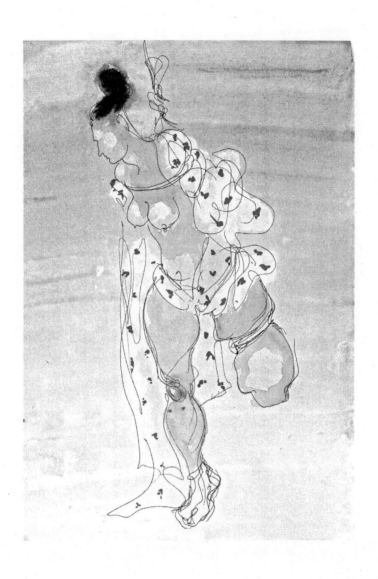

213

Theresa May pleaded with Conservative MPs on Monday not to tie her hands in Brexit negotiations in Brussels, as party whips hoped they had bought off Tory rebels ahead of 48 hours of potentially knife-edge votes in the House of Commons.

Financial Times, 12 June 2018

During his absence I had not been unhappy. Being invited to other people's houses had given me a feeling of superiority, as I compared their insipidly pleasant state to my own. There was a barrier between them and me, invisible but impassable like the invisible bars in modern zoos, where the tropical animals are confined within their ground by a space of heated air.

At the same time, I knew that they in turn would have been uncomprehending if they had known that my contentment came from a man who was able to say, 'I shall hold you for ever, because I shall always find new ways of torturing you,' and that my own particular paradise of the green fitted carpet, the blond machine-carved furniture, and the pressed-glass vases was paradise only because I did not dwell there of my own free will but was held in bondage there.

Edith Templeton, *Gordon*, Olympia Press, 1966

Oh bondage, up yours!
Oh bondage, no more!

Poly Styrene for X-Ray Spex, 1977

TITANIA:
Come, wait upon him; lead him to my bower.
The moon, methinks, looks with a watery eye,
And when she weeps, weeps every little flower,
Lamenting some enforced chastity.
Tie up my love's tongue, bring him silently.

Shakespeare, *A Midsummer Night's Dream*

Whatever diminishes constraint, diminishes strength. The
more constraints one imposes, the more one frees one's self of
the chains that shackle the spirit.

Igor Stravinsky, *Poetics of Music in the Form of Six Lessons*,
translated by Arthur Knodel and Ingolf Dahl,
Harvard University Press, 1947

The Bracelet: to Julia

Why I tie about thy wrist,
Julia, this silken twist;
For what other reason is't
But to show thee how, in part,
Thou my pretty captive art?
But thy bond-slave is my heart:

'Tis but silk that bindeth thee,
Knap the thread and thou art free;
But 'tis otherwise with me:
I am bound and fast bound, so
That from thee I cannot go;
If I could, I would not so.

Robert Herrick (1591–1674)

Round field hedge now flowers in full glory twine
Large bindweed bells wild hop and streakd woodbine
John Clare, *The Shepherd's Calendar* – June, 1827

Unwilling lovers, love doth more torment
Than such as in their bondage feel content.
Lo I confess, I am thy captive I,
And hold my conquered hands for thee to tie.
Ovid, *Amores* 1.2, translated by Christopher Marlowe

There was a sharp burning pain in my groin, where my harness was digging in under tension. The ropes were tangled round my body. Above me they stretched in a tight line towards dark rocks. I tried craning my neck to look up but could distinguish no human shapes – just a slender thread attached miraculously to something on the mountain. There was still no sound – just a bleak, grey emptiness. I seemed to be suspended in some gloomy limbo, alone and deserted. I wondered whether the others had been pulled off – whether they were all dead, or unconscious from terrible injuries, powerless to rescue me from this overwhelming sense of abandonment.
Stephen Venables, *A Slender Thread*, Hutchinson, 2000

November 21.

My Nightmare

There is always something which drags me back from the achievement of my desires. It's like a nightmare; I see myself struggling violently to escape from a monster which draws continuously nearer, until his shadow falls across my path, when I begin to run and find my legs tied, etc. The only difference is that mine is a nightmare from which I never wake up. The haven of successful accomplishment remains as far off as ever. Oh! make haste.

> W.N.P. Barbellion, *The Journal of a*
> *Disappointed Man*, G.H. Doran, 1919

And every poet has some Muse from whom he is suspended, and by whom he is said to be possessed, which is nearly the same thing; for he is taken hold of.

> Plato, *Ion*, translated by Benjamin Jowett, 1871

A thin karmic thread winds between us, linking us through something the poem holds that is true to this moment. But a karmic bond that consists of such a very tenuous thread is scarcely, after all, a burdensome matter. Nor is it any ordinary thread – it is like some rainbow arching in the sky, a mist that trails over the plain, a spider's web glittering in the dew, a fragile thing that, though marvellously beautiful to the eye, must snap at the first touch. What if this thread were to swell before my eyes into the sturdy thickness of a rope? I wonder. But there's no danger of this. I am an artist. And she is far from the common run of woman.

> Natsume Sōseki, *Kusamakura*, 1906, translated by
> Meredith McKinney, Penguin Classics, 2008

GARDENER:
Go bind thou up young dangling apricocks

> Shakespeare, *Richard II*

But if, baby, I'm the bottom,
You're the top!

Cole Porter, *You're the Top*, 1934

Held by the ropes, my body stands without a ground.
It falls, but does not fear any impact.
It experiences the illusion of Life without the promise of
Death.

Marika Leïla Roux (Gorgone), study-on-falling.com

Models and riggers: Unnamed; Ada La Venom, page 158; Ada La Venom (model) and Osada Steve (rigger), page 16, page 18 (upper), page 23, page 121; Ayumi LaNoire, page 44; Billie Rose and Dry Sin, page 150, page 152; Cad and Phoenix Flight, page 162, page 171; Denisse, Whiterabbit and Udo, page 38, page 61, page 100, page 164, page 177, page 199; Federica Laquartacorda and Andrea Quartacorda, page 83; Gorgone and Nina Russ, page 8, page 185; Isabell TeCosa and Koikunawa, page 213; Kitty Rea and Maxim Kalahari, page 146; Kitty Rea and Nina Russ, opposite epigraph, also page 79, page 154; Laura and Davide 'MaestroBD' La Greca, page 108; MaYa Homerton and Andrea Ropes, page 71; MaYa Homerton and Miss Eris, page 18 (lower); Miss Bones and Fred Hatt, page 28, page 214; Niyouli and Arnoys Nicolas, page 197; O.c. Harddwn and Fred Rx, page 218; Rija Mae, page 127; Sasha and Gestalta, page 36; Skinny Redhead, page 173, mentioned page 130, skinny-art.co.uk; (from left) Sophia Rose, Miss Bones and group, page 220; Tenshiko and Kirigami, page 20; Zlata and Red Lily, page 35, page 216.

With thanks to Nina and Aidan – BiZarre Events London (page 55, page 63, page 72).

CAUTION

Please do not try shibari without instruction.

Some of the more louche settings implied or drawn in this book are not shibari venues but part of a more varied club context.

TRAINING

anatomiestudio.com (Anna Bones and Fred Hatt)
A-Nicolas.art (Arnoys Nicolas)
laquartacorda.it/en/nawame (Andrea Quartacorda)
Oxford Rope Bight (Phoenix Flight and others/FetLife)
shibariclasses.com (Nina Russ and Bruce Esinem)
shibaristudy.com (Gorgone and others)
studiokokoro.co.uk (Clover and Wykd Dave)